FOOTPRINTS

One night a man had a dream. He dreamed he was walking along the beach with the LORD. Across the sky flashed scenes from his life. For each scene, he noticed two sets of footprints in the sand: one belonging to him, and the other to the LORD.

When the last scene of his life flashed before him, he looked back at the footprints in the sand. He noticed that many times along the path of his life there was only one set of footprints. He also noticed that it happened at the very lowest and saddest times in his life.

This really bothered him and he questioned the LORD about it. "LORD, you said that once I decided to follow you, you'd walk with me all the way. But I have noticed that during the most troublesome times in my life, there is only one set of footprints. I don't understand why when I needed you most you would leave me."

The LORD replied, "My precious, precious child, I love you and I would never leave you. During your times of trial and suffering, when you see only one set of footprints, it was then that I carried you."

Author Unknown

Eric Steinhardt...Artist

ONLY ONE SET OF FOOTPRINTS
AN
INSPIRATIONAL AUTOBIOGRAPHY

921
Ko

ROSEMARY KOENIG

DEDICATION

This book is dedicated to my four children: Mary Lou Maher, Jack, Harry and Dan Koenig. They have laughed and cried with me for over forty years of our struggles together.

Their loyalty sustained me through the difficult years and their love nourished me during the lonely years. I thank them now for my seventeen grandchildren and seven great grandchildren who are the fringe benefits of my life story.

ACKNOWLEDGMENTS

An enormous "Thank you" to my dearest friend, Helen McSloy for her many hours of editing and typing this manuscript. Without her generous assistance and moral encouragement this book would never have been written. It is a better book because of her valuable suggestions. Helen's compassion has caused her to become deeply involved in the lives of the residents of the Shelter of God's Love. Her concern for my Shelter family has freed me from any anxieties about them while writing this book. She is one of God's greatest gifts to me and only He can thank her for all she has done.

A special note of gratitude to my dear parents, brothers and sister who took from me the hurt of rejection and replaced it with their love. Thanks also to my in-laws, Harry J. Koenig, Msgr. Harry C. Koenig, Dr. Charles Kramer and Mary Rach for their loving concern for the spiritual and physical needs of my family. Thanks also to my nephews, Chuck, Bob, Jack and Tom Kramer, J.B. and Dan Rach and to my niece, Kathy Staley. They are all VIP's in the story of my life.

I thank God for His answer to all the prayers that have been said for the success of this book, and I thank the people who have interceded to Him on my behalf.

Appreciation is extended to the dear Missionary Sisters of the Sacred Heart whose hospitality provided me with the serenity needed to write. My story has been written in the natural beauty of the Cabrini Retreat Center and in the sublime and holy atmosphere of their Foundress, St. Frances Xavier Cabrini. Sisters Ilaria, Camille, Mary Ann and Adele made my stay with them a very happy experience. Phyllis Becherer, the secretary at the Center was very accommodating and her many kindnesses added much to my comfort and enjoyment.

In all undertakings there are many individuals who are seldom mentioned but are important to the success of our endeavors. At the retreat center I was loved and cared for by the Gambino family - John, the custodian, his wife Maria, the cook, and their two darling daughters, Nardina and Josephine. They, along with the other cook, Domenica Bellissimo pampered me and kept me well nourished while writing this book.

A special "Thank you" to my volunteer assistant director, Katherine Scheib who taught me all I needed to know to put this book on computer for the printer.

All of the above are "Behind the scenes" co-authors of this book.

TABLE OF CONTENTS

PART ONE: MY FAMILY LIFE

Chapter

PART TWO: MY INVOLVED LIFE

Chapter

PART THREE: MY LOVE LIFE

Chapter

INTRODUCTION

WHY I WROTE THIS BOOK

In response to those who have asked me why I would undertake to write my first book at the ripe old age of 73, my answer can only be, "I had nothing to write about until now." During the past year the urge to write has been as strong as was my desire to open a home for the handicapped after retirement.

God doesn't whisper when he wants something done; He shouts into the ears of those who will listen. He shouted and I listened. From the beginning to the end of this story He was loving me, protecting and guiding me through the mountains and valleys of my life. The path was at times lonely and frightening but along the way I met Him in His people who brought me His strength, His solace and His unconditional love.

I have walked and talked and worked with God's poor - His lonely and forgotten elderly, His handicapped and little children - and because of them I have had a foretaste of the joys of heaven. People have become my hobby and through their sufferings and joys as well as through my own, I have found a stairway on which I ascend to meet my God.

May this simple story of the struggles and joys of a single parent family encourage you to trust God in your difficulties. Let Him carry you until that day when you will know Him as your personal Savior and can walk alongside of Him in love and adoration.

GOD, THE FATHER, GUIDED ME

My Family Life .... Part One

Chapter 1

CHRISTMAS, 1944

The people were happy, the stores were gaily decorated, the coins were dropping into the Salvation Army kettles, and carolers filled the brisk air with their happy songs of the season. It was Christmas, 1944, in Kalamazoo, Michigan. Gladness and laughter surrounded me and my eight-year-old son, Jack, as we walked hand in hand, isolated from the joyous crowd. My husband had recently left me and our four children. We were shopping for a much-needed overcoat for Jack to wear to Chicago when we would visit Grandma and Grandpa for the holidays. At home was Jack's nine-year-old sister, Mary Lou, tending her two younger brothers, Harry, six and Danny, two.

The melody and beautiful words of "Silent Night" brought me peace, but, also, unrestrained tears. Jack and I drew strength from each other in the firmness of our handclasp. He seemed to sense how much I needed him for I'd notice him from time to time glancing up at my tear-stained face and, saying nothing, he'd just squeeze my hand a little tighter. He seemed to feel that he was now the "man of the house." What a burden to place on such a carefree little fellow. I often wondered if my husband knew the hurts and heartaches he inflicted on his little ones.

My life seemed over because my marriage had ended after what I thought were ten happy years. I now know the truth of the statement, "the wife is the last to know." Loving my husband and believing in the sanctity of matrimony, I was bewildered, ashamed and lonely. My hurt too deep to express, my children too young to fully understand, and — they had their own loneliness to endure.

Mary Lou, who loved her Daddy very much (she was his only little girl) froze all her feelings in being independent of any need of him. She frequently reprimanded me, saying, "Why do you cry for Dad? He didn't want any of us, so why should we want him?" Not wanting her to become bitter, I replied, "When he did want us, he was a good father, and that is why I'm crying. I know that someday he'll remember how much he once loved us."

Harry was deeply hurt, but unable to express it. His silence hurt me. He was aways "Harry Dangerfield" to his father and Harry was happiest when he was "horsing around" with him. Harry's

1

sensitive nature and his inability to express grief always concerned me. It was too bad that this child of six had to be so hurt by one he loved so much.

Danny was too young to realize what had happened. For some time after his father left, Danny continued to sit each evening on the curb in front of our house waiting for his Dad to come down the street and carry him into the house on his shoulders. It was a long time before he stopped waiting. So many little behavior patterns now became haunting memories for us all.

After a few months of self-pity and despair, I looked to God and begged Him to help me. He heard and answered me. He placed my hand in His and His love and companionship strengthened me. While not immune to the frailties of my former self, nor protected from the sorrows of life, I was fortified by my trust in Him.

Our Christmas visit with my family in Chicago renewed my deter-mination to put together the broken pieces of my life. But what should I find upon returning home — the pipes had frozen — plas-ter was falling from the ceilings — and much of the basement was under water. Somehow there seemed always to be a crisis in my life that negated the luxury of self-pity. The month of January was spent restoring the house to its former livability.

Things were quiet until February when Mary Lou was rushed to the hospital for an emergency appendectomy. My heart ached for her. In the fear of the surgery she was facing, I knew she would like to have had her Dad with her, but she wouldn't admit this desire, even to herself. Open wounds take such a long time to heal.

My neighbors took the boys for the night, and another neighbor and her husband drove me to the hospital, remaining with me until the surgery was over. I stayed with Mary Lou all night sitting on a chair next to her bed, feeling her pain as if it were my own. Upon my return home at noon the next day, I was served a subpoena. My husband, unaware of Mary Lou's surgery, was seeking a di-vorce, interest in our property, and custody of our four children.

I immediately contacted my family in Chicago. My brother referred me to a Christian attorney in Kalamazoo. Before seeing him, though, I talked to my pastor, Msgr. John R. Hackett, a kind, gruff old Irishman who reflected the God he served in his compassion and justice toward all of God's people. Monsignor was a very sick man, terminally ill with a malignancy, but always available to his parishioners. Msgr. Hackett helped me to know how I could with God's help, enjoy caring for my deserted little family. Everything that happened from that day on has made me aware of God's presence in my life and how He used His people to help me.

Since there is nothing but brokenness in a divorce, I shall not dwell on the suffering and hurts of all parties involved. Let it be understood that no one comes through the court action of a legal separation without scars — scars that can only be healed by the power of God's love. The dissolution of a marriage is even more difficult to understand when a partner, attempting to lead a double life, is overly attentive and loving in order to conceal illicit relationships. I wondered how I could have been so dumb. (I like to think it was not so much my stupidity as it was my husband's superior acting ability.) Because of a divorce, family life is disrupted, children are hurt by the division of loyalty to parents they love; parents suffer from the stigma of rejection and failure. Because of the strong negatives, equally strong positives had to be pursued to rebuild a sound and healthy family structure. A new personality developed in me when I stopped thinking of myself and began thinking of the children our marriage had brought into the world. Their needs superseded mine, and in my desire to meet those needs, I found happiness and fulfillment in all the struggles and joys of my new life.

Our home in Kalamazoo was everything I had always dreamed of — big, old-fashioned, with a white picket fence surrounding the lawn, garden and play area. But my joy and pleasure in it ended with the divorce. It was sold and we moved to Chicago to begin a way of life I had never envisioned — I thought our marriage would last forever.

Late that summer, Mary Lou (the little mother of our family) and Danny went to Chicago where Grandpa and Grandma Rach met them at the train station. Jack and Harry, my protectors, remained with me until the following day when all the tangible assets of my shattered dream were placed in a moving van and a home once again became a house inviting a new family to find love and shelter in its embrace. I wanted a new beginning, but more than anything else I wanted to keep the past always with me — not the sadness, but the memory of the love I once had for a man I could now pity more than condemn.

On the day after my arrival in Chicago I reported to the Board of Education for a battery of qualifying tests for a job as a school clerk.

On Tuesday after Labor Day, a shell of my former self reported for duty at Willard School. I had no self-confidence, I was unaccustomed to working outside the home, and my heart was heavy thinking of my four little ones left at Grandma's. During my lunch hour I called home to find out how Danny was doing. The others were in school — they would be busy enough to forget me, but my little Danny — his heart must be broken without "Mommy." It was with mixed emotions that I heard Gram say "Danny has been fine. He hasn't mentioned you all morning." It was disappointing and hurtful to learn that I no longer was the center of his life, but still I was thankful for my wonderful mother who loved and cared for my children as she had cared for her own.

Even though I had passed the tests for appointment to my position, I felt very ill-prepared for my new career as a wage earner and head of household. My co-worker was a black lady named Helen Garnett, who, because of superior ability and many years seniority, was my guiding light. Working under her direction I sprouted from a frightened nothing to a happy human being. To laugh again, and be accepted by my co-workers was a sense of God's love for me. In the isolation of my loneliness, God's love flowing through His people comforted and strengthened me. I didn't know it was God. I just said "Thank you" to His people.

Chapter 2
FRIENDS AT WILLARD SCHOOL

Helen Garnett was one of the most inspirational persons in my life and one of my dearest friends. Long before the days of Civil Rights this gallant lady was crusading against the injustices suffered by her people. Her approach was different from that of the militant leaders who have followed her. More than once I saw my friend annoyed at the lack of interest many teachers had in their pupils — teachers, through whom children were getting their first glimpse of a world outside their homes. Helen often said that if she were a teacher, she would try to inspire the very loftiest ideals in her pupils. "I would encourage them with little prizes at the end of each week for the children who came to school looking the neatest," she said. "Others would receive little rewards for coming to school with their homework prepared." She often spoke of the encouragement children receive from their adult models. Not by civil disobedience did she wish to excite them, nor by maudlin lamentation about the sorrowful lives which had been inflicted on them during the past hundred years. No, Helen Garnett would teach them by example to prepare themselves for acceptance in the society to which she knew they belonged. If fear and indolence represented the image of Blacks, then that image had to be replaced by one of self-respect and goals. My good friend had all the respect that anyone, regardless of race, could bestow on her. She was an honorable, lovely lady. Her color gave her no special acclaim, nor did it deny her any recognition that was rightfully hers.

One of the things I most admired about Helen Garnett was her sense of justice. Being one of ten white persons in a school of two thousand black children and forty-eight black teachers, my minority role was clearly defined, but caused me no problems, for Helen was my friend. When black parents enrolling their children were rude to me, my soft-spoken co-worker would arise from her desk saying, "I'll take this one, Mrs. Koenig." She would then tell the parents, "Don't talk to Mrs. Koenig like that. She's asking questions that need to be answered and doesn't have to take your abuse." I felt secure in the knowledge that Helen was my friend. She taught me a very important lesson. Being a certain color doesn't make you right or wrong, but being a human gives each of us the right to be accepted for WHAT we are, not for WHO we are. If you knew Helen Garnett as I did, you loved and respected her and wanted to do nothing that would hurt her or her race.

Many of the teachers at Willard were as great an inspiration to the children as Mrs. Garnett wished them to be. I recall one teacher, Mary O'Neil, who taught a first grade class. She taught as Helen wished everyone would teach. Because of her love for the little ones, she called forth the best that was in them.

I remember, too, an adjustment teacher, Marguerite Kirkling, who worked with children having difficulties. Marguerite accepted each frustration of her pupils as a frustration of her own. She, too, contributed much to my knowledge of black people. I met this lady later when I was at the Christopher School, and my friendship with her continued until her death in 1964.

Marguerite had a little son named Charles. I remember the day Marguerite and Charles came to my brother's wake. Dan, with his bristly, straight, crew-cut hair was a strange sight to Charles as he rode with us from the funeral parlor to my home. He kept fingering Dan's head trying to find out what made his hair so straight. Finally, when his curiosity got the best of him, he asked Dan, "What's the matter with your hair? It's funny." The question, though unanswered, amused us all. In those days we didn't really have a chance to know each other. Blacks and whites lived in our own little neighborhoods and outside of business, rarely saw one another. This is a sad commentary of our day. We missed a great deal.

When I lived in my parents' home, a lovely black woman ministered to the needs of our family. She was a typical Southern mammy who showered kindness and love on the ones for whom she worked and with whom she lived. We all loved Bernice, but not in the same way as I loved these other women who were on a higher rung of society, education and influence than I was. They didn't have to be kind to me. Perhaps that is why I cherish the memories of their thoughtfulness.

Chapter 3

DOUBLE TROUBLE

When we first came to Chicago, we lived in the second floor apartment of my parents' building, where they occupied the first floor. My brother, John, and his family lived on the third floor.

One of my brother's sons, Dan, along with my Dan, both age three, were successors to the old Katzenjammer Kids comic strip. Two inspired little devils, living in the same building spelled trouble, especially when their minds were keen, their bodies agile, and their parents exhausted. The person who introduced us to tranquillizers, I'm sure, must have encountered these two dynamos along the way and recognized the need for sedation.

Their entertainment one day consisted in removing the spotless laundry from the clothes line and hiding it in the alley. It took a little time before all the pieces were located, put through the second cycle of the non-automatic washer and re-hung on the non-automatic clothes dryer - the clothes line. Two little fannies were crimson that night but their spirits were undaunted. They both enjoyed a good night's sleep which put them in the driver's seat when the dawn broke on another day.

The following morning before breakfast, our two little "innocents" were playing in our paved yard. While climbing up the stairs from outside the rail, Dan K. reached out for the clothes line on which he wanted to swing. It was too early in the morning to be well coordinated so he missed the line and went head first onto the cement. When his screams broke the sound barrier, I ran to him. At the sight of blood around his head and eyes I feared the worst. Once again, the protective arm of his over-worked and under-paid Guardian Angel shielded him from disaster. Even though his eye looked like that of a Cyclops and his forehead was swollen, bruised and bleeding, he was not seriously injured. His grotesque face would have made a wonderful Halloween mask but it was three months too soon to be used for that purpose.

The game they played was known only to themselves until one leg was encased in a plaster cast. The inquisition as to how anyone in his right mind could jump out of a second story window led to the disclosure that the game they played was "Super Man." Danny K. in hot pursuit of Danny R. chased him up the front stairs of their apartment building. Danny R. to avoid capture, jumped through the open stairway window. (He admitted later that he thought he was on the first floor when he jumped). When he found himself in mid-air, he knew that a mistake had been made, but it was too late to change the direction of his fall.

In the kitchen was hung a behavior chart on which was recorded each child's conduct for the day. "I hung up my clothes" — "I didn't fight" — "I obeyed my mother," etc. were sometimes the cause of more friction than serenity as the children would question one another regarding the integrity of each one's reporting. Many a time I'd get a call at work asking me to disown a dissenter or find one less resident when I returned home. One day Dan called to question Mary Lou's authority when she ordered him to stand on his head in a corner for half an hour as punishment for some infraction of house rules. Mary Lou's authority was supposed to be indisputable, but in this case, Dan's sentence was commuted by way of a phone call seeking clemency. "Ma Bell" was a fairly good mediator, but not as effective as "Ma Koenig" in person after working hours.

Chapter 4
LETTING GO

Everything was going well until December, 1945 when Mary Lou was hospitalized with acute rheumatic fever. God shook my complacency once again and drew me nearer to Him in my pleading prayers for her recovery. She recovered completely with no apparent heart damage.

My first year in Chicago was the most difficult one. There were so many adjustments for us, and for my dear parents who opened their home and their hearts to us. In the adult lives of our children, parents are expected to stand at a distance and physically help them, but remain emotionally aloof from their trials and sorrows. My mother and father felt my loneliness as much as I did and they helped me to accept my life as God willed it. They gave me enough sympathy to let me know they understood, while impressing upon me the gravity of the tasks that lay before me. It was difficult to work all day and in the evening begin another day's work at home. I was assuming all the responsibilities of married life, but enjoying none of the companionship and the joys associated with it. The friendships of married couples I missed especially. I belonged to neither the single nor the married society. My friends, always loyal to me, included me in their parties and I frequently was a guest in their homes, but being in the company of our former friends intensified my loneliness. Often I'd just close the blinds on a Saturday night and pretend that everyone went to bed when their children did. I was very tired so this kind of fantasizing wasn't too difficult for me.

My goal was to make up to my children for the loss of their father. My longings, my loneliness and my confused life were submerged in family responsibilities. At night I'd cry alone. Cry for the love I had lost and cry to my Heavenly Father for the strength and comfort of His love. Both loves have always been with me, but the love for my husband changed to pity. As the memories of that love faded, the love of God was made more apparent in my life and became the axis upon which my life rotated.

Chapter 5
ST. JOSEPH'S ACADEMY

One day my mother spoke to me about sending the two older boys to a very fine military school near Chicago. She was afraid I would not be able to keep up the pace at which I was working. If the boys were away during the week, the laundry, meals and housework would be lessened. The boys could come home each weekend and I probably would enjoy them more on weekends than if I had them at home all the time. The thought carried with it the hurt of another separation from members of my family. It seemed as though there was so little that I was able to cling to and enjoy. But I knew my mother was right so I went with her to inquire about enrolling the boys at St. Joseph's Academy.

It always seemed that when I was feeling the sorriest for myself I met people whose kindness brought the presence of God close to me. So it was at the Academy in LaGrange where I met a kind and understanding nun named Sr. Liguori, the Principal of the school. Her gentleness inspired my confidence. I knew my boys would love her and that I had found a friend in her. The goodness of God was reflected in her face.

Many of the students were from one-parent families while others had come from very normal, well-adjusted homes. The boys looked so sharp in their uniforms, Sr. Liguori so beautiful in her attitude, and they all seemed so happy, that I decided to enroll my boys.

During the summer months I worked in a neighborhood ladies' apparel shop, and all the time I was not waiting on customers I spent sewing name tapes on the clothes of my young cadets. This was not a chore I enjoyed. I detested sewing and felt that each tape sewn was hastening the day my boys would be leaving. I didn't want to earn a living for my family so that I could pay others to raise and enjoy them. However, this was exactly what was happening.

The day after Labor Day when I came home from work, I had supper with the children, borrowed my father's car and drove Jack and Harry to LaGrange. It was a very sad and quiet drive to the Academy, but the ride home without them was almost more than I could bear.

It was late when we arrived at the school and the other boys were asleep in the dormitory. Through the darkened room, I cautiously followed Sister Bernadette to the boys' beds. Jack was ten years old so he couldn't cry; but Harry was just eight and couldn't help crying and calling out, "I want to go home with you, Mom!" His tears and his pleading tore me apart. I could hear nothing else all the way home. The tears that fell almost blinded me andI know that God was my co-pilot that night. I knew I'd miss my boys, but I didn't expect my soft-spoken little Harry to be so unhappy. The next day, Mary Lou, Danny and I began a school year without the laughter and responsibility of our two little guys. I wasn't sure the lesser work and worry would offset the happiness they had contributed to our family. Little boys have such tenderness for mothers and I needed their love. We endured the lonely week, but the three of us looked forward to the weekends when Jack and Harry would be home. We were a proud and happy family when they were home, especially when we were being escorted to Sunday mass by our two cadets in their military attire.

Chapter 6
GRANDPA'S WAKE

My father, a medical doctor, had not been well for some time, but had continued to go to his office daily. The day came, however, when he was no longer able to take care of his patients. He was sicker than any of them.

It was on December 6, 1946 when my father was taken to the hospital and before dawn on December 7th he had passed away. His death was difficult for us to accept as we hadn't realized he was so ill. His death was mourned by many as he was one of the last of the old-time family doctors. He had been a practicing physician and surgeon on the south side of Chicago for more than forty years.

Since my father had no tolerance for fancy funeral parlors which were just being introduced to our society, he had requested burial from his home. Because he owned his own three-apartment building in which his family were the only residents, the entire building, including a beautiful English basement was available for the wake.

The first night of the wake, one of my friends called me aside to tell me that my sons in their military uniforms and my nephew, J.B. Rach, were the fore-runners of the Andy Frain ushers. They were meeting people in the vestibule as they entered the building and before the guests even went to the first floor to pay respects to my mother, our three miniature doormen were inviting them to join others in the English basement where cigarettes, cigars and coffee were on the house.

As the mother of four children, I had disciplined myself not to be surprised at anything that kids did, but I must admit being a bit shook-up at this. The services of our ushers were immediately terminated and they were confined to quarters, even though I know my father would have enjoyed his grandsons' final tribute to him. My parents adored their grandchildren, and in the close proximity of our shared lives, our family ties were indestructible.

Chapter 7

A CLOSE CALL

The following weeks were busy, but happy ones. I met wonderful nuns as well as fine parents at St. Joseph's Academy. The classes at that time were held in portable buildings and each year the parents sponsored a dinner to raise funds for the building of a new school. We enjoyed the camaraderie of working on the dinner and sharing our dream of a new school building.

It was while working at St. Joe's that I met Brad, a very interesting and kind man. He was a widower whose son was in class with one of my boys. I found myself wishing we could work on the dinner every evening so I could be with him. He was good company and had a great sense of humor. Since our feelings for each other were mutual, we knew that platonic friendship was not going to work for us. Some of the good nuns, not knowing I was divorced, were promoting our friendship and encouraging marriage. They thought we would make a good couple. I thought so too — but my church saw things a bit differently. I remember the roses Brad sent Mary Lou when she was graduated from elementary school. They were beautiful and it felt so good to know that this man I admired thought enough of me to remember my daughter in such a nice way. How-

11

ever, Mary Lou's reaction was different. Her comment was, "I don't want any flowers from him. The flowers are awful." I guess she saw in him a threat to the solidarity of our little family. Children at that age are not too concerned about the happiness of their parents if it might jeopardize their own position and comfort. However, my mother's love and concern for me was unselfish and always reassuring. Her love penetrated all our lives, not just in words, but in service.

One day, while sensing my indecision about remarriage, Mother talked to me about my plans. She said, "I understand your loneliness and the hurt you have suffered, and I wish things could be different for you, but you must think things through. You cannot remarry and continue to receive the sacraments. Does Brad mean that much to you?" My heart answered "Yes" but my mind said "No." Brad's love and attention were a real tonic for my bruised ego, for he assured me that I was capable of loving and being loved once more. He told me of his love on that Father's Day when he introduced me to his family. I, too, loved this man so the inevitable had to happen. I had to make a choice. I've never regretted saying "Goodbye" to my dear friend, Brad. It was just a case of a good man losing out to the Best Man, and Brad didn't mind being the loser.

Chapter 8

WE VISIT OUR NEW HOME

After my father's death, Mother moved to Washington, D.C. to live with my bachelor brother, Bill. Our apartment building was sold, so, using the cash salvaged from the sale of our house in Michigan, I made a down payment on an inexpensive little house in Chicago. I thanked God for that money, for I was not the most attractive tenant — a single parent with four small children, three of them boys! In fact, I doubt if anyone would have rented to us.

The house was not yet ready for occupancy, but one day while visiting my sister, Jo Kramer, she suggested that we take the children, her four and my four, to see our future home. Her suggestion brought a wild scramble for seats in her station wagon. Before I could even consider the idea, the car was filled with eight eager beavers ready for the expedition.

When we arrived at our unfinished house, the eight children, my sister and I climbed through the paneless windows and thrilled at the beauty of the skeleton of a house soon to be our home. After the tour, bodies were piled into the station wagon for the journey home.

Later that afternoon, one of our prospective neighbors called to ask if I was missing one of my children. It happened that Jack had been left behind while prowling through the house and we hadn't yet missed him. My neighbor thought it would be nice if I would reclaim him.

It was with considerable embarrassment that I introduced myself to my new neighbor and claimed my prodigal son. I hurriedly explained to her that only four of the eight children were mine and only four would be moving into the house being built. I didn't want her to consider selling her house before we even moved in to ours.

Chapter 9

MARY LOU BAKES JACK'S BIRTHDAY CAKE

Our new house was purchased in June for occupancy in August and it needed to be painted and decorated before we moved in. On the Fourth of July, Jack and I tackled the job. I had borrowed my brother's car and since it was Jack's 11th birthday, Mary Lou was in charge of preparing the birthday dinner. She was just 13 months older than her brother but a very capable little girl. I could depend on her to fix as nice a dinner as any adult.

Since we had no communication between the two buildings, the time of the dinner had to stand and we had to be there as scheduled. We arrived only five minutes late and I was surprised to find Mary Lou already taking up the dinner and placing it in the warming oven for us!

The meal consisted of delicious fried chicken, frozen peas, a salad, mashed potatoes and the fanciest birthday cake you have ever seen. The frosting was a bilious blue on which was placed a vivid American flag in red, white and blue frosting. I can't say it was the most appetizing-looking delicacy, but it did thrill Jack and it warmed my heart to know I had a little girl who tried so hard to make a birthday happy for her brother. The cake was made from one of grandma's recipes. This was long before the days of cake mixes. I was mighty proud of my little 12-year old daughter, who so willingly and aptly accepted responsibility.

Chapter 10
OUR NEW HOME

When we moved into our new home in August, 1947, our work began. We spent the first month clearing the debris from the lot. The house was an inexpensive one and not much more than a shell, but it gave us a sense of pride — the kind felt only by those of us who think the soil around our home is almost gold dust because it is a spot of earth that is our very own. It doesn't have to be elaborate.

We all had a hand in the landscaping. I remember raking through rich, black dirt, then spreading creeping bent grass over it. For this job we were all in our bare feet, and like the little old wine makers stamping the juice out of grapes, we were pressing the grass into the dirt. The children thought it was great sport. Kids have an affinity to dirt and they loved it when I wet the dirt down and they wiggled their toes through the mud. At any rate we got the job done and were proud of that lawn for many years.

The sidewalks consisted of flag stones which were spaced from the back door to the alley. About two years later, Jack tackled the first of his many man-sized jobs around the house when he set forms and poured a concrete sidewalk where the flag stones had been placed. He was only thirteen years old when he made a success of this undertaking. I marveled at the ability of this young fellow, and as the years went by, his many talents put to good use, added much to the value and comfort of our home. It wasn't until he joined the Navy at seventeen that I realized how much he had been doing. He took as much pride in his home as any man would have taken. I was glad that one of my sons had inherited his father's talent and skill in the mechanics of being a home-owner.

Chapter 11
GRANDMA'S INVITATION

At Thanksgiving time Grandma sent us the train fare for a visit with her in Washington, D. C. Needless to say, it was a real treat and the children thoroughly enjoyed the ride through the mountains. We felt very "upper class" as we visited Grandma in her beautiful apartment hotel. My memories of the train ride, however, are not so pleasant, for on that journey I was to learn the hard way, that crime does not pay, even though one gets away with it.

Dan was just five years old and since he was small for his age, I smuggled him on the train without a ticket. (Not exactly an honorable thing to do, but I confess to having done it.) No one questioned his age, but I wonder now about my own elastic conscience that was so conveniently stretched.

Dan was a lovable little extrovert who talked to everyone and had a way that was appealing to all. He'd get into friendly conversations with the other passengers, and even though he had been coached to say he was four years old, there was a little bit of the bravado in him. He wanted to brag about being five, so every time I saw his mouth open I wondered what was coming out of it. It was a long and frustrating ride from Chicago to Washington, D.C. waiting for our little time bomb to explode.

It was while I was in Washington that I received a wire from Chicago telling me that I had passed the Civil Service Exam for School Clerks and would be certified in that position in the near future. Certification meant I would be transferred from Willard. It was with mixed emotions that I thought about leaving my friends at the Willard School.

Chapter 12
TRANSFER TO CHRISTOPHER SCHOOL

Many events put a life together. We become whole only when our emotional, physical and spiritual experiences complete the jigsaw called, "Our time on earth." Certain memories remain with me even though many years have passed since I was transferred to the Christopher School for Crippled Children. My years there enriched my life and those experiences are some of the tiles of the mosaic that is my life today.

At Christopher School there was an unusually large staff. In addition to the principal, teachers, physical therapists and school secretaries, there were bath attendants, crippled children's attendants, bus, physical therapy and lunchroom attendants. I mention all this to show the great number of people needed, each contributing in his or her own way, to attain their shared goals — the education and well-being of handicapped children. Many of the staff had known tragedies in their own lives and with or without a formal education each was working out his or her own salvation in service to others.

At Christopher School I learned that the only remedy for the ills of our society is God's love flowing through us in compassion for others. Happiness cannot be purchased; it must be earned and derived from others. It is like a ball which comes back to us only when we throw it to someone or against something. At Christopher School I saw humanity portrayed at its very finest. The veneer of people sometimes wore thin when exposed to the sorrow and happiness of those little ones who seemed to have been forgotten by God. As we worked with them, we found God's grace and His love. There was the usual amount of pettiness, fault-finding and unhappiness, but those who felt God's love in the smiles and contentment of His little afflicted ones were richly rewarded.

It was a strange lesson that I learned from Marianne, a beautiful little three-year-old armless girl, through whom God taught all of us how to love Him. One would have expected such a handicap to embitter the parents and be a part of the body of an arrogant, spiteful brat. Instead, the disability made this little one an angel without wings. When, as a nursery student, a rhythm band bracelet was placed on Marianne's ankle, it was far more interesting to the other children than the ones placed on their wrists. So Marianne, without arms, became a leader in nursery school when all the children wanted to be like her and have their bracelets put on their ankles rather than on the arms which God had given them. This is only one example of Marianne's courage instilled in her by the inspiration of her parents' acceptance and love.

Another family with two adorable little sons suffering from muscu-

lar dystrophy was an inspiration to all as they radiated love, tolerance, patience and all the other virtues which most of us strive a
lifetime to acquire. The mother and father were very active in the
Parents Association and always were willing to assist in any way to
alleviate the sufferings of other children and parents. Little Stevie
was the younger of the two boys. His arms and legs were hardly
bigger than a sparrow's. His beautiful smile turned attention away
from his handicap to the beauty and radiance of his goodness. No
bitterness — no anger; only love as manifested in the innocence of a
child's smile when God seemed to be in back of his transparent
little face. The older boy, Skippy, was as beautiful and lovable as
his brother. In fact, the staff had loved Skippy so much that Stevie
had no trouble following in his brother's footsteps. The love and
benevolence of this family cut a pathway through life wide enough
for them to walk six abreast. The six included the parents and two
able-bodied sisters. There was such a beautiful bond of love in that
family that I have never forgotten them.

Another child I remember with great tenderness was a seven-year-
old boy severely crippled by arthritis. Michael was unable to get out
of his wheelchair, but from that wheelchair he reflected the miracle
of God's love in his smile which was an inspiration to all the able-
bodied persons who passed in front of him. A word to little Michael was always received with a smile that felt like a benediction.
One morning as I was sitting at my desk, the phone rang. The
caller reported that Michael had died during the night. Unasham-
edly I wept as I took the message to my principal. The entire school
shared the sadness of his death. We all had lost one we loved.

I recall a humorous incident when Marie, a little black girl stopped
me in the corridor and, with a smile as broad as her face, asked me
how I liked her new leg. I stopped while she pulled up her slacks
to show me the prosthesis. I admired it, and knowing that artificial
limbs sometimes irritate the wearer, I asked how it felt. Her response was, "It feels good, but I don't like the color. They gave me
a mahogany leg when they know I'm a light oak." No complaint
about the wooden leg; just a gripe because her all-important femi-
nine vanity, at age nine had been injured. She could manage the
inconvenience of a wooden leg, but she didn't want her beauty
marred.

An incident that shook me out of my complacency was the time an
eighth grade boy was brought into the office. I was minding my

own business while the principal, truant officer and others involved tried to shake this boy's determination to run his own life and his own limbs. I was shocked to hear the principal exclaim in a loud voice, "You wear your arm every day, and don't ever come to school again without it." I was amused at the words of the admonition but I thought of the annoyance it was for some pupils to be told to bring a note to school for an absence. Here was a boy being told to bring his ARM! I breathed a prayer of thanksgiving that my own little ones didn't have to be reminded of such a thing.

No wonder I had courage to face my own problems. I just had to work hard and trust God to help me overcome any feelings of loneliness or despair that might cause me to falter in my determination to make a happy life for my fatherless children. His presence became so real to me that I found myself talking to Him quite frequently throughout the day, just a little "Thank you, God" or a simple prayer, "God help me." I needed Him and He was the unfailing source of my strength.

Chapter 13
WAGS

In our own home, we did not feel as secure and safe as we had been in the apartment building with people above and below us. The children wanted a dog and I thought we needed one for protection. I don't recall where we got Wags, but I do remember that many times I wished he were back where he came from. Our life with Wags was very trying. He had an insatiable appetite for human flesh. Everybody who entered our house was greeted by this mongrel's show of teeth. I threatened to get rid of him every time I saw one of Mary Lou's friends (he liked girls) on my kitchen table, ashen with fear as the dog tried to get at her. I sent at least three children a week to my brother-in-law, Dr. Kramer, for medical treatment for dog bites.

One day, upon arriving home from work, I found another child at my front door reporting a dog bite. I found Wags and let him feel the heel of my shoe. I had intended to shove him but he lost his balance and went down the basement stairs. In so doing he broke his leg. Wags knew I was sorry for what had happened so he hobbled in front of me with the thump of his leg in a cast, reminding me constantly of my cruelty to animals. I did not mean to hurt him. I was upset, however, by the pain he was inflicting on little children. The cast clumping around the house seemed to be saying, "Look what you did, you devil, you."

About a month after the cast was removed, he again started his attacks. Again, the parade of his victims to my front door. Finally I reached my limit. I borrowed my brother's car and with Dan as my companion, took Wags to the Humane Society. Dan was very upset about losing his dog, but once we had relinquished Wags to the kind man in charge of the place, he felt better. Going home he said, "That man was so nice, Mom, I know Wags is going to be a better dog there. He just doesn't like our friends."

Wags was soon replaced by a darling little puppy who came into our home and quietly but permanently captured our hearts. She was named "Dusty" because of the looks of her after a nap under the boys' beds.

Chapter 14

DUSTY VISITS DAN

When Dan was seven he was hospitalized for a month with mononucleosis. While he was in the hospital, I visited him daily, but the one he really wanted to see was his faithful little canine friend, Dusty. This mongrel dog played an important role in our lives for many years. I asked a nurse who was working on Dan's floor to bring him to the window the following day when I would bring his dog to the parking lot for him to see. For obvious reasons, I must omit the nurse's name, the name of the hospital and that of the good nun who broke a few rules for the sake of a lonely little boy separated from his dog. Miss Friendly told me to hold off awhile for she thought she could come up with a better idea — and let me tell you, she did. She told me to bring Dusty up to the fifth floor by way of the fire escape, and since Dan was in a ward, she would see that he was taken to a private room at the end of the floor where Miss Friendly's patient, Sister Kindness was confined. The plan called for Miss Friendly to meet me at the door of the fire escape and smuggle me and Dusty into Sister's room. The plans were simple, but the actual maneuvers were a bit different.

Most people, and that would have to include myself, have had little experience walking up five flights of open iron railings with a forty pound dog tucked under a winter coat. I know Dusty was scared, but "Yours truly" thought I'd die before I ever reached the top. The dog seemed to know that everything we did was being done for a purpose, so she kept her mouth shut all the way up the fire escape, but once she got in the hospital room where she saw Dan, we had to gag her. Dan embraced his dog and Dusty seeing her friend once again howled loud yelps of joy in response to his hugs and kisses.

We couldn't let the patients know of Dan's rendezvous with his dog sister, so the visit had to be cut short. The hospital room used for our tryst was occupied by a beautiful lady who had been one of the strictest of nuns while in her position as Director of the School of Nursing. However, the poor woman, while waiting for the inevitable end to her suffering from cancer, enjoyed the fun of such a prank. None of us is too dignified or too righteous to forego the joy that comes from stooping to help a little child.

When the visit was over, I started down the fire escape with purse under my arm, dog under my coat and bats in my belfry. I was paralyzed at the sight of the great expanse below those open steps. Dusty and I had to get down so I prayed my way to the last step and it was not until I reached terra firma that I thought the visit had been a good idea. The joy it brought to Dan was worth all the inconvenience. Dusty returned home, crawled under her friend's bed and was reconciled to the fact that Dan had not walked out on her. She was happy once again.

Chapter 15
HARRY'S BURNS

The school bells had dismissed all of us for the summer. It was a dark and dreary day — that first Saturday of vacation. A general let-down was felt by all. Mary Lou and I were cleaning out our bedrooms. It was a day for putting away the winter clothes and getting our summer wardrobes in order. All the boys were out.

Mary Lou and I had enjoyed a nice bacon sandwich for lunch. The skillet was still on the stove when Harry came home with a ravenous appetite for some lunch. He liked the smell of the bacon so he decided to settle for a bacon sandwich.

Harry was old enough to fix his own lunch. He had done so many times before. Using the same grease left in the pan, he cooked bacon for his sandwich. When the bacon was cooked he removed it from the pan but forgot to turn off the electric stove. After awhile he smelled the grease burning. Knowing that turning off the stove would not stop the burning, he tried to remove the skillet from the burner. It was an iron frying pan which retained the heat. Harry lifted the handle. The heat was so terrific that he dropped the pan spilling the hot grease on his arms and chest. I heard the most frightening scream and when I got to the bottom of the stairs, I saw Harry rolling on the floor trying to get some relief from the excruciating pain. I rushed to the phone, called my brother Bill who came immediately and drove us to the hospital. I sat with Harry in the back seat and felt every pain he was feeling. There was nothing I could do to console him, even though he begged me to help him. I had a blanket wrapped around his arms to keep the air off the burns, but that was all I could do. He received first aid at the hospital, was given a sedative and sent home with both arms bandaged liked a mummy. He lost the use of his arms for about six weeks. Everything had to be done for him. With the help of his two brothers to dress him, and assistance at the table from Mary Lou and me, he survived the inconvenience.

Every fourth day Harry had to return to the doctor to have the bandage changed. One of his visits to the doctor's office was on the fifth of July. As we sat on the bus listening to all the comments about his bandaged arms, we were conscious that he was an object lesson to all the children as a horrible example of the tragedy of fireworks. The burns were bad enough to bear, but the conclusions drawn by the on-lookers was an insult to Harry's intelligence. Hot bacon grease which caused the burns had dignity compared to having been burned by forbidden fireworks. Harry dreaded his visits to the doctor for it was torture to have the bandages changed. After six weeks of such suffering, the bandages finally were removed, but his activities still were restricted.

This boy who had loved sports and lived to participate in them could no longer do so. Because of the possibility of infection, Harry had to become a spectator for six months while his arms were healing. The curtailment of any outlet for the energies of this young, spirited colt made him a very angry boy. It hurt me that this little fellow who was so kind that he could hurt nothing or no one had to endure such pain himself. In Harry's sight even a mouse had a right to live, as did all insects even the ones that tormented us. Harry and his friends often caught fireflies and placed them in mason jars with holes punched in the top so they could be kept alive. Harry never kept his captives any length of time. He interpreted this as cruelty. He was very discerning about the realities of life. I worried about the shallowness of his protective coating, knowing he was vulnerable to hurt by a world not sensitive to his feelings.

Harry returned to school in September with the restrictions still binding. He was forbidden to take gym or engage in any active sports even though the bandages had been removed. This situation was tolerated just so long — then all the pent-up emotions came to the fore. He refused to study, he annoyed his teachers, he was nasty to the boys, and in general was an arrogant, bold little brat. I knew this was rebellion against his restricted life, so I worked with the teachers and promised to support them by refusing Harry permission to come home week-ends until he cooperated with them and respected their authority.

As Jack was unpacking his clothes for his week-end visit he sadly relayed Harry's angry messages to me. "Tell Mom I don't care if I never go home again. I like it out here better than home. I don't miss anybody." Such verbal abuse from my hurt little son caused me much pain. I cannot describe my reaction to his comments, except that I knew his anger was being expressed out of the frustrations he was feeling. Harry had placed a shield around himself that no one seemed able to penetrate.

I wrote him a long letter pleading with him to behave so he could come home 'cause I missed him very much even if he didn't miss me. I told him over and over how much I loved him and wanted him home. I wasn't sure my "poor Mama" appeal would help, but it did. After a few days I received a beautiful note from Harry in which he told me that he would be good 'cause "I miss you, too, and I miss your home 'maid' cooking." I think he missed the meals more than he missed me but at least it was a break-through to this rebellious little boy. He did have feelings and I still was able to reach him.

Not too long afterwards he came home and as time went by his restrictions were lifted. When he was able to "run with the pack" he became, once again, my darling little Harry.

Chapter 16

FISHERMAN JACK

"**M**a, can I go fishing tomorrow at Sherman Park?" A simple question got a simple answer. "Yes." Bright and early the next morning Jack and his friend Mike were seen walking to the bus with a bag of lunch in one hand and fishing pole and bait in the other. All was right with their world. At nine o'clock that night my eyes filled with tears as I recalled the sight of the two excited boys and the bounce in their steps as they walked to the bus. At four o'clock (the time both were supposed to be home), I saw Mike on his paper route with his "business as usual" strut. "Where's Jack?" I asked. "I don't know," said Mike. "The last time I saw him was about three o'clock. We weren't having any luck where we were fishing so Jack looked for another spot. I don't know where he went, because I couldn't find him when it was time to go home."

Panic seized me as I phoned my brother John to tell him of my fears. He responded immediately and the two of us drove through the park searching for clues to Jack's whereabouts. After about an hour we reported his absence to the police who put me into the back seat of their squad car and took me on a scavenger hunt for the remains of my boy. THEY were looking for empty lunch bags or other tangible evidence of Jack's presence in certain areas of the park. I was looking for the body, period. Since that day I have felt the utmost sympathy for parents who in similar situations endure such torture and must accept, the inevitable fact that tragedy has struck. We did find Jack's empty lunch bag and the police noted the spot for future search down into the deep. When darkness put an end to our search we started for home with the assurance that if Jack did not come home before morning, the lagoon would be dragged. It was with a heavy heart and sore, red eyes that I returned to my brother's car for the journey home.

At the intersection of 79th and Racine, while waiting for the traffic light to change, who should we see, standing on the corner, but a tired, dirty moppet who resembled my missing fisherman. Mixed emotions tore at my heart. My angel son — my devil son. My brother stopped the car and honked the horn at the character on the corner. Jack recognized the car and knowing he was in the dog house, reluctantly came across the street. He was carrying no fish, but I am sure he was cooking up a good fish story to tell his frantic mother. When he saw my expression of anger, however, his fish story had about as much substance as the fish he didn't catch.

Jack had inherited, I suppose, his father's love of fishing. Time was of no concern to a dedicated fisherman, but to the fisherman's mother, anxious about his safety, time was indeed measured. Perhaps only a day had passed since the start of this escapade, but to me, it seemed like a lifetime. Uncle John, the one in charge of our search expedition waived all punishment but had a heart-to-heart talk with his young nephew. My brother was what is known as an 'easy mark' with kids, so he just told Jack that women worry and must be placated to a certain extent if men are to live happily in the same world with them. This meant no more days of complete disregard for the concern mothers have for their children.

Chapter 17
HARRY'S PAPER ROUTE

When Harry was in seventh grade he transferred to Little Flower School to be with his brother, Dan, after his original sitter, Mary Lou had graduated from elementary school. What I recall most of all about that time was Harry's paper route.

Every morning at 5:00 a.m. he would start out on the route with his dog. I never had to awaken him, or in any way remind him of the time. He'd get up, fold his papers tuck them into his paper cart and start out with his loyal Dusty following close by. Dusty seemed to feel as responsible for the route as did Harry.

One morning, when the temperature was ten degrees below zero, Dusty came to my bedroom and barked until I got up to see what had happened. Looking out the bedroom window I saw Harry walking down the street. He had not taken Dusty with him. I opened the door and Dusty, running like a greyhound, soon caught up with her friend. Harry stopped to pet her, then lifted her into his paper cart. When they returned home Harry explained that he hadn't taken Dusty because it was too cold for her. But Dusty never missed another day after that because Harry always kept a woolen blanket in the cart for her when the weather was bad.

Dusty and Harry had many friends on the route. Kind, elderly ladies who served hot chocolate and rolls to Harry and treated Dusty to dog yummies and bones. Dusty knew where their friends lived and often would run ahead of Harry to pick up the loot. They would stop at these friendly oases and then start out again, warmed by both the treats and the graciousness of these good women. I never met their friends, but I did say many a prayer of thanks for their kindness to my son.

Harry had his route for over a year, but when he started high school it was more than he could handle. He had a long trip to school and a lot of homework which prevented his getting to bed early. He told his boss he was going to give up his route at the end of the year. At Christmas time Harry received $95.00 and his dog received a hand-knit sweater and several boxes of dog yummies.

On Christmas Day, the snow was so heavy that all traffic was halted and I wondered how Harry would be able to get through the streets to cover his route. He placed his papers on a sled and tried unsuccessfully to get them delivered. Finally, Dan and I bundled ourselves up and joined him. The snow was still falling in a real blizzard. I had a babushka around my head, and looked like a kook to the dressed-up folks on their way to Christmas services. Danny pushed the sled as I pulled it and Harry delivered the papers to the doors. The way he felt about his customers, Harry never could have disappointed them, but he was very glad when the last paper had been delivered.

Upon arriving home, the three of us took hot baths, changed our clothes and felt more like joining our friends in the trek to church. When Mary Lou saw the outfit I had worn as a paper woman, she looked aghast and said, "Mother, you didn't go out looking like that?" She had yet to learn that a mother's pride is often sacrificed to help her children.

Chapter 18
OUR FIRST CAR

A s the children grew older and bigger, our house became older, but smaller. I guess houses age like people do. I once was a tall five foot young lady, but now, in my golden years, I have to wear very high heels to reach my former height. The children needed some stretching space so I decided to have a garage built for additional storage area with a patio attached for recreational purposes.

Our house was on a corner so it was necessary to get a driveway permit. Arrangements were made with the contractor to acquire the necessary papers and to begin construction of a two-car garage before I had even one car to put into it. My neighbors thought I was a little wacky, but they were kind and neighborly, always ignoring my many idiosyncracies.

My thoughts of ever owning a car were as distant as the proverbial "pie in the sky". The shopping bags used to transport groceries to feed four growing children were becoming heavier each year and I learned that two bundles of roof shingles could not be brought home on a bus. While my sub-conscious mind was thinking of a car, my conscious mind responded to the ring of the telephone. The caller was my sister, Jo. "Would you be interested in buying my car?" she asked. "Bud is getting me a new one and this old Dodge is too good for a used car lot. She deserves to remain in the family. If you want it you can have it for $300." I thanked Jo for the offer saying I'd think it over and get in touch with her later in the week. Would the reality of a car available to my young males stir up more trouble than joy? Could I afford the insurance? the license plates? etc. In those days the money remaining after pay day put no strain on my wallet. None was hidden under rugs, none placed in savings accounts, none set aside for emergencies. In a situation like mine, you just couldn't have emergencies, and if you did they couldn't cost anything.

In a conversation with Dan, I asked his opinion regarding a car in the Koenig household. He told me that they (my children) were planning to surprise me with a car at Christmas and had been saving their money expecting to pay a lot more than $300. He said that they already had that much money and to get the car. He talked with the others who were away from home and they all contributed their savings toward my early Christmas present. When my brother, Bill, heard of the gift, he said, "If the kids are buying the car, I'll treat you to the first year's insurance."

I have always felt that the Blessed Mother answered my daily rosary in this way, for in the foreword of the novena booklet, it states that Our Lady intercedes to her Son for that which she thinks we need most. I never thought of praying for a car, but I'm sure that is what I really needed and wanted most. Even my neighbors began to believe that my unseen sponsor (the Good Lord) was providing for me.

Chapter 19
PATTY, MY FIRST GRANDCHILD

In our work areas, we establish relationships with friends who become as much a part of our lives as if they were family members. Never as dear to us as our immediate family, but in the sharing of tears and joys we establish friendships which are like pillars to which we cling tenaciously for understanding and love. Little ones do not understand the heartaches and the little fragments of happiness to which adults cling in their struggle with life. Children make our work and worry worthwhile, but they cannot offer us the graciousness of a tender friend who understands and helps us. In my friendships, I have always felt the peace and joy of God's love.

So it was among my friends at Christopher that I anxiously awaited news of the birth of my first grandchild. I wasn't much good to the school that day, as my mind was on Mary Lou, my own little girl who had grown up so fast and was now going through the pains of childbirth, so that she, too, could know the ecstasy and joys of motherhood.

Finally, the long awaited call came from my son-in-law, Jerry. "Hi, Grandma," he said, "You have a beautiful, healthy little granddaughter. She weighs seven pounds, has a full head of blond hair and is as beautiful as her mother." After congratulating him, I brought him back to earth with the plebeian question, "How's Mary Lou feeling?" His response was typical. "She's doing great and so am I." I knew further questioning would get evasive answers because Jerry was enraptured with the joys of fatherhood. More than anything else I wanted to rush over to the hospital to see Mary Lou and our new little family member. However, mothers and new-born infants had to be kept antiseptically clean and grandmothers with all the germs of the world in their pores were not allowed to visit them.

The new parents were alone, but together, as they stepped across the threshold of freedom to a bondage of love for the new little life that was being entrusted to their care. The thrill of such an experience can only be equated to the love God has for His children when He permits them to share with Him the beauty of creation.

All this elation was felt by Mary Lou and Jerry as they saw and held the tiny life their love had brought into the world, but the feelings that grandparents have at such a time is indescribable. How can a grandchild be graphically described with only 26 letters in the alphabet? No matter how you assemble the letters, the words are inadequate. The beauty of a baby can only be compared to the grandeur of a mountain, the inspiration of a sunset, the beauty of Spring's budding greens, and the brightness of moonlight on darkened waters. My little Patty, though, defied even that grandiose description. She was my very own granddaughter - my own little girl's baby.

Christopher School tolerated my insanity that day and shared with me the thrill of my new title, "Grandma Koenig." I still delight in the title even though Patty is now the oldest of seventeen grandchildren and seven great-grandchildren.

She was the only grandchild born while I was at Christopher School. It was the first time in my life I could claim such perfection as my own, and all I had to do to achieve such success was to raise my Mary Lou to be such a wonderful wife and mother.

Chapter 20

FLORIDA

It was October, 1961 when my brother Bill offered me an all-expenses-paid vacation in Florida. He planned on going there after Christmas and asked me how long I could be away from my job. Since there always was a week vacation at Christmas time, I knew I could count on that and then perhaps another week on my own time, so, without hesitation I accepted his wonderful offer. I had heard about the beauty of this southern State and had always hoped to see it.

It was exciting and thrilling to shop for clothes that would be needed for the trip. I felt like a kid anticipating a visit to Disney Land, and I thanked God for Bill who was offering me such a wonderful vacation — which was to be the first of many.

The expectation was great, but the reality was fantastic. To be transported by plane away from Chicago's snow and sub-zero temperature to Miami's 70 degrees, dry and sunny weather was a tonic beneficial to all, but especially to one who couldn't afford it.

As Bill went to the car rental desk, I stood watching the travelers and the many people who had come to meet their friends and relatives alighting from the never-ending parade of landing planes. The slow, indifferent attitude of the natives walking through the airport in summer clothes was a delightful change from the hustling and tensions of the bundled up travelers I had left behind at O'Hare airport. When the paper work for the car rental was completed, Bill gave me the keys to a beautiful new Bonneville which I was to drive to the Key Biscayne Hotel. As I drove out of the airport I rolled down the windows so I could breathe in every bit of Miami's invigorating air. It was 11:00 p.m when our plane landed, but in Miami, (the city that never sleeps) people were filling the hotels, restaurants, and other attractions as though it were early evening.

Our vacation was one of complete relaxation. The pace of life was moderated to accommodate the pleasure of not having to BE anyplace, and not having to DO anything. Two weeks to enjoy the luxury of leisure, removed physically, mentally and emotionally from the pressures of survival.

Being a morning person, I arose earlier than Bill and headed for the dining area on the hotel patio where I'd enjoy a gourmet breakfast amidst the sunny breezes, the swaying palm trees and flowering shrubs. It was a scene far removed from my customary ''breakfast on the run'' for the family at home. Our early afternoons were spent on the golf course and later in the pool, after which we returned to our rooms, showered, rested and dressed for a night on the town. The evening would begin with the delight of a sumptuous dinner in the hotel dining room or in some elegant restaurant in or around Miami, after which we'd take off for the Jai Alai games or the dog track. (A brother and sister team did not participate in the "moonlight and roses" routine.) Bill and I both liked the games and the races. I liked them, especially, since Bill gave me all my gambling money. If I won or lost it didn't matter. It was like playing with Monopoly money. It was such fun to be extravagant for a couple of weeks during those frugal years.

Looking back on these luxury vacations, I thanked God for the heavenly respite from what was, at that time, a busy and uneventful existence. It seemed as though God was giving me a taste of all the "goodies" to be measured against the value of His love and all the inner joy and peace such love had given me. Comparisons were odious, but by this time I knew I had the better of the two life-styles, for God had begun to fill all the voids in my life with the power of His love.

Chapter 21

ONE PARENT — FOUR TEENAGERS

The title of this chapter spells DISASTER for both the teens and the single parent. I cannot dwell too much on the explosive combination of the above, but I can thank God that with His help, we all survived.

Rules had to be made and strictly enforced, for how else could a family, supposed to be "normal" live in such an abnormal atmosphere? During the adolescent years children assume the intelligence of professionals, while acting out the roles of pre-schoolers. There is no rhyme or reason for their behavior. They are so wise and yet so crazy. They really don't want to be the way they are — they don't know why they do the things they do. The rebellion of teen-age children is something all families must suffer through. It is a time when their obnoxious behavior is the most difficult to accept, that young people need an abundance of love and reinforcement. As a single parent, with no one to backup my discipline, I had to be really tough; sometimes cruel and heartless in my enforcement of the rules. I didn't want to be strict, but these negative reactions were brought forth when confronting my rebels who hung together through thick and thin. I was the monster they had to handle. Oh, yes, they loved me — but really didn't know why, and I loved them and wondered why.

I remember one incident in which Harry, my quiet, well-behaved son fell off his good behavior rocker, and with his friend decided to mark the bricks of an apartment building with obscene 4-letter words. The owner of the building who had been given Harry's name as the culprit called me. Confronted with what he was accused of doing, Harry admitted his guilt. His punishment consisted of carrying a pail of hot water, soap and rags about a mile back to the building where he, under the supervision of the owner, washed off all the graffiti. Harry thought it made more sense to get the water from the building owner rather than carry the dumb pail a mile with water in it. I preferred the water from our house as I knew the weight of the water was a lesser inconvenience than the embarrassment that went along with it.

Then there was the time Jack decided he didn't feel like weeding the garden as he had been told to do. When I saw the spade standing upright in the dirt with no sign of Jack around, I began looking for him. Two anxious hours later, I received a call from a priest friend of Jack's who interceded for him to be able to return home minus the firing squad he thought might be waiting for him. He was received back into the fold, but was introduced once again to the spade and the weeds he had deserted. He was grounded for a week.

Dan was small for his age and two years ahead of his peers in grade placement. Being the friendly little extrovert that he was, his objective in school was to be socially, rather than academically accepted by his classmates. As a result I was called to the principal's office quite often to give one good reason why Dan should continue to remain a student at St. Ignatius High School which he seemed to think was a play-pen rather than a school. His pranks were too numerous to recount, but at seventeen when he entered the Jesuit Seminary, he walked into the office of the Novice Master and was greeted by Father Clear, who had been his prefect of discipline at St. Ignatius. Father said to Dan, ''You are the last person I'd expect to find here.'' Dan replied, ''That goes double, Father.''

Mary Lou was not as hard on my nerves as the boys, but she, too, was a teenager. One of her bright ideas was to invite her elementary school graduating class to a party at our house. The party was all right, but I knew nothing about it until the guests started arriving. Yes, you guessed it — the guests went home, but much anger and hostility filled the air around our house that summer evening. The witch was flying without her broom.

Mary Lou recently reminded me of her craziness as a teenager when she was suffering from delusions of being a famous designer of clothes. She practiced her non-existent talent on my meagre wardrobe. I'd stumble upon the futility of her efforts when I'd be getting dressed for work. Where once a dress had been hanging, I would find only half a dress. Mary Lou had cut off the bottom half to make herself a skirt. When she discovered the task too great for her ability the skirt would be hidden in a vacant lot in back of our house. My wardrobe was practically depleted before she accepted the fact that she couldn't enlarge her wardrobe by devastating mine.

We both laughed as she recalled this behavior, but I assure you there was no humor in it at the time. The experience was non-profitable in every way. Mary Lou is now a nurse, not a designer of clothes, even though she wears them with great style.

For the encouragement of those who are presently living through these difficult times, I'd like to conclude this chapter with words written by one of my children on a Mother's Day card. "Thank you for not having given up on me during some trying years. It is the curse of parents to learn from experience what grief they caused their own parents a generation earlier."

Not one tear was shed in vain, not one hurt too deep to heal, for I enjoyed my four children and today am proud of every one of them.

Chapter 22
ONE DOOR CLOSES — ANOTHER DOOR OPENS

Another move, another break with an established pattern of life. My children were raised, the house that once was filled with laughter and tears, celebrations and graduations was now an empty nest. It was over, and once again I cried a little, trusted a lot and stormed heaven for divine assistance as I began another walk into the unknown. At the time of my divorce my children took my mind off myself and called me to a surrender of self that gave me the fortitude to face a future for them. Now I was really alone — my children were gone. I wasn't aware of God's presence at this time, for I had yet to meet the God I know now. Even though I prayed to Him, trusted and loved Him, I knew Him only as my Heavenly Father who had called me, as a Catholic, to pick up my cross and follow Him.

After a few months of loneliness living with memories that caused pain, I made the decision, with God's help, to move on to another phase of my life. My home was sold and once again I started on another unchartered course into the future.

Everything no longer needed was discarded. That had to include all those treasured snap shots of the children, all their little notes with misspelled words, "When I grow up I'm gonna mary you." — "When I get big I'm going to bye you a big car then we can go for rids in it to the country." All these precious souvenirs had to be reread and wept over before being thrown away. One envelope was kept for each child. In them I put pictures and notes they might want to keep for their own children. Everything else went out. One of my sons, witnessing the maudlin procedure, with an attitude of cold emotion said, "Ma, why don't you just throw everything away without reading and bringing back memories that make you cry?" "Just let me enjoy the luxury of one last good cry before I leave all this behind," I replied. A new life was beginning again and anything that hurt or kept me from moving on had to be destroyed. My mind told me to move on, but my heart said, — "Linger awhile."

Even though I knew I could not continue to live alone in a six room house, moving to a small apartment from a house in which I had lived for seventeen years was a traumatic experience. Not only was I leaving my home, I was moving from one side of the city to another. In Chicago, that is almost equivalent to moving to another town. Everything about my future was frightening.

At the time of my move I was working at the Foster Park School with a wonderful group of teachers. God, however, seemed to be telling me not to get too attached to persons or things. He called me to trust Him to fill all the voids of such detachments. How little I knew then of His love, but I see all of it now as the fulfillment of the Promise of Faith that He gives to all who bring Him their burdens.

During these first seventeen years in Chicago many things happened that could have destroyed me if it weren't for my trust in God's power and love. During that time I lost both of my parents, a brother who was like a father to my children, and my father-in-law who helped me with the financial needs of my family and supported me with his love. It seemed as though God was removing all my props. It was over once again — not my life — just that part of it that centered around my children.

Feeling free as a bird I moved to the north side of Chicago in 1965 but like an addict in need of a fix, I began looking for new responsibilities. I had been helped in my difficulties by people God had called to help me. Now He was calling me to help others. He filled the empty nest of my heart with His compassion and love, then asked me to give it to others as it had been given to me.

Chapter 23
INSTRUMENTS OF GOD

Before concluding this story of my family life, I want to thank all those people who were used by God to help me find His presence in my life.

The understanding and help given me by my dear parents, sister and brothers, as well as that given by my in-laws cannot be described. They constantly gave of themselves and were supportive of me always. We had many good times together and much of my strength was derived from their love.

Because I received no support money from the children's father, my father-in-law gave me a check each month to help with the cost of the boys' tuition at St. Joseph's Academy. After Grandpa Koenig's death, Msgr. Harry Koenig, (Uncle Father, to my children) continued the financial assistance that had been given to me by his father. (When the children were small they never knew quite how to address their priest-uncle. Sometimes they'd call him Father, sometimes Uncle. They finally decided on "Uncle Father" which they call him to this day.) The children's college expenses came from money inherited by Msgr. Koenig when his father died. He told me at the time that the best investment possible of his father's money was in the education of his grandchildren.

Two of my sons graduated from Notre Dame University, one from DePaul University and my daughter graduated from St. Francis School of Nursing. God not only provided them with the cost of their schooling, He provided all of my children with the intelligence needed to achieve their goals. I was beginning to understand the meaning of Divine Providence.

A friend, indeed, was Msgr. Hackett, who guided me through the distressing period of my divorce.

Another very dear friend was my blind high school classmate, Dorothea Jennings, now a nun living in the Monastery of the Precious Blood in Canada. Her many beautiful letters inspired me to seek God's help during my trials. Her words encouraged me to find the comfort of God's presence in my oppression.

I am grateful to all those people who allowed me to lean on them until I was able to stand alone. Thank you, God, for each and every one of them.

JESUS, HIS SON, SAID, "FOLLOW ME"

My Involved Life .... **Part Two**

Chapter 1

A STEP INTO LUXURY

The move from my south side home transported me to the luxury of a beautiful high rise on north Lake Shore Drive. The apartment had been chosen by my brother, Bill, whose life style was much more elegant than mine. As the founding producer of three summer theaters, Bill had developed a taste for the niceties of life — always enjoying and sharing them with many of us. Our magic carpet, however, was pulled out from under us when the failure of his theaters impoverished Bill. I enjoyed my fling at affluent living, but such luxury became a burden when Bill was without income and no longer able to help. He left Chicago and went to his alma mater, Georgetown University in Washington, D.C. to look for work.

It was at this time that I moved to a smaller, less ornate apartment very near the one in which we had been living. It was a large and beautiful one-bedroom apartment on the 11th floor overlooking Lake Michigan to the east and the city and its beautiful sunsets to the west. I was intoxicated with the beauty of the moonlight on the lake. The "man in the moon" seemed to be laughing at my astonishment as I viewed its awesome splendor and radiance.

The water surged like shimmery oil through the fluorescent streams of moonlight as if it were playing hide-and-seek with the darkness of the night; its ripples, like a swarm of fire flies attuned me to the beauty of creation. It was a fleeting moment, however, for soon the moon would take its light to another part of the city and once again the lake would become invisible. It seemed that my life was like that — the vast unknown of a lake hidden under the darkness of night. I, too, had my moments of glory and glistening fulfillment, but they seemed as fleeting as the moon's rays on the blackened waters of Lake Michigan. That night I asked God to let the light of His love reflect His image in me in the same way that the moonlight brought forth the beauty of the water.

More comfortable in my own middle income surroundings, I became excited about my new life. It is strange that financial security never contributed to my happiness, except where it could be used to draw me closer to my family and friends. The comforts brought into my life because of money, developed in me a great need to share them with others. I loved my nice apartment, but never enjoyed it more than when entertaining my handicapped friends or my small grandchildren. The kids thrilled at the fun of throwing bottles, cans and papers down the incinerator — or riding the elevators for a few fun-filled moments.

God was generous with His many blessings and I remained close to Him in the sharing of His gifts. I could only give what He had given me — but He gave so much. How really poor are those whose security rests in financial assets or tangible property. Possessions are too superficial to satisfy the deep craving within all of us to be loved and respected for what we are, not for what we have.

Chapter 2
APOSTOLATE OF THE HANDICAPPED

One of the ministries of the Archdiocese of Chicago is the Apostolate of the Handicapped — a city-wide outreach to the disabled. It is geographically divided into two north and two south side units with approximately two hundred persons in each group. The Apostolate is under the supervision of Father Charles Kelly and other priests who are the spiritual directors. The work is performed by lay people who elect their own officers and unit directors who are responsible for the planning and logistics of the monthly pilgrimage to different host churches in the Chicago metropolitan area.

On the first Saturday of each month volunteer drivers provide transportation for handicapped adults to attend a pilgrimage to a designated host church where the Liturgy is celebrated, luncheon served and entertainment provided. Volunteers from the host parish assist the disabled in whatever way they can — from helping them to and from their cars to serving them their lunch. It is a beautiful "coming together" for both the disabled and the able-bodied. None of the Apostolate volunteers receive any financial reimbursement for their expenses. In fact they pay for the privilege of serving by contributing a specified amount each month to help defray the cost of the Saturday lunch. Following the entertainment, all join in the recitation of the rosary which climaxes the day's activities.

I had heard of this group long before my move to the north side but was unable to volunteer because of family obligations. Now I was free — free to return to my first love, that of working with the handicapped. In 1965 I became a volunteer driver for the Apostolate of the Handicapped, and my life was enriched through my association with them.

One incident, I remember, portrayed the stamina and beautiful attitude of an 80-year old passenger of mine who lived alone in a small apartment in a housing project. Nellie had neither legs nor thighs. She was a mere torso who had to be belted into the front seat, then supported by a weighted pillow in front of her. The children and parents in Nellie's neighborhood shopped for her and assisted her in other ways that allowed her the independence of living alone, at the same time giving her the support and companionship of people who cared about her. She was a gregarious little lady, loved by everyone. One day while driving Nellie and two other women to church, the passengers in the backseat were quite vocal about their arthritic pains, particularly the pain in their legs. We listened and sympathized for a while, then Nellie, with a smile on her face, turned to me and said, "I never thought that being without legs would be a blessing, but I guess it is because I'll never get arthritis in them." My backseat passengers got the message and were silent.

Our first Saturday outings brought us all so much pleasure that I added to our regular schedule a couple of luncheons at my apartment. Twice a year some of the handicapped and volunteer drivers would gather at my apartment for a luncheon that began at noon and ended at 10:00 p.m. when the guests reluctantly started for home. These were really fun times and we always set the date for the next luncheon before the first one ended.

By sharing my God-given gift of mobility with the disabled I found rewarding friendships and deep satisfaction. I received much more than I gave, for God taught me to use the wealth of Divine Providence with abandon. He always had more to give.

Chapter 3
SCHOOL TRANSFERS

Even though I moved from one end of the city to the other, I continued to travel a round trip of 20 miles a day rather than leave Foster Park School where I had been working for the past eight years. Foster Park was the school in my old neighborhood, so my ties were not only to the faculty, but also to my neighbors and their children — ties too strong to break. Friendships are so meaningful when lives are shared in the intimacies of suffering and joy. I knew they would always be my friends, but I did not want to leave them. God, however, had other plans. He didn't want me to crowd my life, even with old friends, for He had new ones for me to meet.

So, after three months of being a north side resident working in a south side school, I transferred to a district office in my new location. I enjoyed my work and my new co-workers, but in the sterile and childless environment of the district office, I missed my little friends. First, I was separated from my own children and now I was removed from my school children. I remained at the district office until I was eligible for assignment to a vacancy at the Lincoln Elementary School where my mental age once again coincided with the chronological age of the students — and I was happy. I especially enjoyed my visits to Nancy Stocking's kindergarten class and Mrs. Waterman's mentally handicapped youngsters who knew me only as the "Candy Lady."

It was to my advantage in the years prior to retirement to work a longer school year, thus earning a larger salary upon which my pension would be calculated, so after five years at Lincoln I moved on to the 12-month Logan Continuation School.

I cannot describe the Logan Continuation School in any other way than desolate. The purpose of this special school was to enforce a state law which required children who had dropped out of school prior to age sixteen to attend a continuation school one day a week. In my opinion, very little was accomplished on that one day as attendance was erratic, courses obsolete and many teachers indifferent to the needs of their students. To paraphrase a question asked many years ago, "Can anything good come out of Logan?" I'd have to answer, "Yes," for it was at Logan that students encountered Tom Benson, the teacher in the Counselor's office. Most of the time Tom's office looked like a doctor's waiting room, wall-to-wall students. Tom Benson inspired confidence in these "losers" and helped them to get jobs, while teaching them the self-discipline needed to keep those jobs. He respected his students and taught them to respect themselves, for in Tom's thinking there were no "drop-outs."

One day a vocal member of the Board of Education stopped by to visit the school. She told the principal that she had seen me the night before at a Board dinner and asked where I was working. He directed her to the Counselor's office where she talked with me and explained the reason for her surprise visit to our building. "I have always been curious about the Continuation School program," she said, "So I decided to have my husband drop me off today while he takes care of some business in the neighborhood." "I am still curious about the program even though I've worked in it for over a year," I replied.

Her first visit to Logan prompted another visit the next day, when she returned accompanied by newspaper photographers in search of a good story. After the second visit, the good (?) story was told in the headlines of our daily papers and the expose' of the school's financial drain on the taxpayers along with the negative achievement of the students forced the closing of Logan Continuation School at the end of that school year. Her visit was the "Kiss of Death" for me as the school staff concluded that it was my criticism of the school rather than her eye-witness account of it that brought about its demise. Their false accusations didn't disturb me for I was quietly thanking God for putting an end to such an abomination.

With the close of Logan I was transferred to the Cook County Juvenile Detention Center, a correctional institution for juveniles, most of whom had been involved in criminal offenses.

My years at the Detention Center awakened in me an awareness of the traps that are enslaving many of our good, but gullible young people. I will tell of one such incident that gives a child's point of view to a situation beyond his control.

Jose, one of the teachers at the Detention Center knew the importance of family involvement with their children at the center. He worked with the parents trying to change the wayward direction of their young people. Frank, one of his students, was celebrating his birthday and his mother, accompanied by Frank's two younger brothers, Steve and Joey, brought a cake to school for the party.

41

The younger boys were not permitted in the classroom area so Jose asked if they could sit at one of the desks in the office until the party was over. "I will be delighted to have the company of such good-looking young men," I replied, and began gathering crayons and drawing paper to keep them busy until their mother returned. However, Steve, the ten-year old, wasn't interested in coloring or drawing. He preferred to visit with me as their desks were adjacent to mine. He poured out his heart to me when he said, "I miss my brother so much that every time I pass by his bedroom and see it empty, I cry." "If you feel that bad your Mom must feel terrible too," I replied. "We all cry," he answered. At this point while fighting back my own tears for this little family, I said, "You must remember all this, Steve, and see that you stay out of trouble when you get big." "I don't want to be in trouble, even when I'm not big," said he. "After school I run all the way home and stay in the house 'cause the gangs try and hurt us. My brother got in trouble 'cause he was afraid of them and they made him do bad things." "Well, Steve," I replied, "Just be a good boy and help your Mom so she won't have to visit you in a place like this someday."

When the party was over, Mrs. Lopez, with eyes red from crying, returned to claim her two little boys. The incident left me with a deep sense of frustration for our families who are living out their lives under a cloud of great fear. Remembering my own happy childhood, I prayed that God would call His people back to Him, by whatever means necessary, for our children are being scandalized, hurt and destroyed by the ruthless conduct of some of their peers.

At the Detention Center I saw, also, the hopelessness of undisciplined youths who struck out at innocent people, victimizing them with criminal attacks on their persons or property. A world without discipline is a world without love and a world without love is a world without God. I thanked God for the many people who reached out and tried to redirect the energies of these young people whose behavior cried out for love and discipline. Many had never known the joy to be found in a loving family structure.

Chapter 4
GRANDMA GOES BIKE RIDING

One of the nicest things about my apartment was its location across the street from Lincoln Park, Chicago's largest and most beautiful park. It stretches along the lake front for miles. Within its boundaries is every kind of recreational facility from playgrounds for the little kids to boating for the big kids, and a wide range of sports, games and picnic areas for all ages in between.

The bicycle path that runs in and out of the park along the lake-front is what I enjoyed most even though I made use of the golf course, the zoo, the summer theater and many of its other attractions. Interspersed throughout the park were several places where rental bikes were available. When my grandchildren were small, they often spent time with me during their school vacations. The highlight of their visits was a bicycle ride through the park followed by a picnic lunch and a trip to the farm in the Zoo.

The first time I suggested a bicycle ride, Patty, age 9, was flabber-gasted at the thought of a grandmother riding a bicycle. She said, "Gram, old people don't ride bikes." (I was then in my early fif-ties.) "In Lincoln Park everyone rides bicycles." I said. "What are old people supposed to do?" "They should rest," Patty replied. Since I wasn't quite ready for resting, I told her, "I'll rest when they throw dirt in my face, but right now, I'm going bike riding. Do you want to come along?" Without hesitation she replied, "I sure do." So off we went on our fun ride through the winding bicycle paths of Lincoln Park, stopping only to enjoy our lunch in a beautiful picnic area where we watched the swimmers and the little ones playing in the sand along the beach. I often used my grand-children as an excuse for my enjoyment of some of the activities that were off limits to sedate seniors living alone. Patty saw many people of my vintage riding bikes that day, so she was not ashamed of Gram on a bike. One time Patty and her sister, Ginny, thought it would be fun to rent a bicycle built for two. It looked like great sport and it was — until the novelty wore off and the fighting be-gan. "Pat, you're not pumping. Gram, make her pump. She's making me do all the work." I'd settle that argument and all would be fun again for a few minutes, when they would crash into some obstacle and another fight would begin. "Gram, she's dumping us on purpose by not steering. Make her stop." When I couldn't stop their bickering, I refereed them back to the bike rental where they gladly returned their tandem bike. They'd never make THAT mistake again.

Mary Lou's children were not the only ones with whom I enjoyed my bicycle rides. Harry and Mary's three children also shared many an afternoon with me. They were older than Patty and Ginny so my rides with them were of longer duration and sometimes more eventful. Especially exciting was the time I lost two of my teenagers, Stevie and Frank. After Ann and I had spent much time looking for her brothers, we returned home to recruit more people to help in our search. Lincoln Park was a big place in which to get lost. As we came into view of my apartment, there were two very dirty and tired young boys sitting on the curb in front of the building. They had taken a wrong turn and lost us in the park. That disastrous turn was followed by a flat tire which forced them to walk their rented bikes back to the stand and then walk the rest of the way back to the building. How glad I was to see them! They lived on the south side of the city and were unfamiliar with the north side, so I was surprised they found their way back to the apartment. When I asked how they found the building, they pointed to the wavy-topped roof on the high-rise next to mine and said, "We just kept our eyes on that roof because we knew you lived across the street from it." I was glad they had been so observant. Teenagers aren't dummies, they just pretend to be.

The zoo in the park was another big attraction for the children when they visited me. I enjoyed it as much as my grandchildren did. Animals and their antics are always fascinating for old and young alike. The Children's Zoo where the little ones are allowed to pet and touch the baby animals is a very popular spot. The trip to the zoo was more of an attraction for my grandchildren than the visit with Grandma, but I didn't mind. I knew they'd be glad to return to my apartment when they got tired. When Dan's family visited from their home in Victoria, B.C., his little ones, Dawn and Deanna were enthralled with the big city. My 11th floor apartment, the lake, the park and playgrounds were their Disneyland in Chicago. Their visit to the zoo was the highlight of their vacation. My grandchildren never ran out of exciting things to do when they visited me. When their energy was exhausted they had fun sitting in front of the windows watching the boats go in and out of the harbor.

Incidentally, I still like to ride a bike in the park and I'm now twenty years older than when Patty thought I was too old for bicycling. I read once that "Age is a matter of mind; if you don't mind, age doesn't matter." I guess I don't mind.

Chapter 5
EDUCATIONAL SECRETARIES OF CHICAGO

Justifiable anger brings about as many changes as "Necessity, the mother of invention," calls forth solutions. Chicago Board of Education school clerks were angry over the attitude of their employers who refused to recognize their contribution to the schools they served. Financial compensation was inadequate and there was little acknowledgement of the quality and quantity of their work. The kindness of many principals and their appreciation for the dedicated service of their school clerks, mitigated some of the difficulties and made the job a rewarding one in spite of the inequities. There were other principals, however, who added their intolerance to the existing hardships.

In every situation there are, and I hope always will be, people who attempt to change the things that need to be changed. Indifference to problems or tolerance of them negates the need for correction so Deloris Adams and Virginia Partee, two long-suffering but vocal school clerks, decided to do more than accept and complain about our working conditions.

Aware of my anger and altercations with the bureaucracy of the Board, Deloris and Virginia, in an effort to improve the status quo, sought my help in setting up an independent organization that would speak for school clerks. To me, it looked like the dawn of a new day even though that day was arriving twenty years after my original certification. I agreed to work with them and after several meetings, we organized and obtained a charter from the State of Illinois for our Association which we called, "Educational Secretaries of Chicago." When it came time to elect officers, I was asked to run for president. At first I declined as the association had been established and developed through the efforts of Deloris and Virginia and I preferred to have them head their own organization. "We are both black and have a good black following," said Deloris.

"We need your color to attract the white votes," said Virginia. Because of my desire to work with my friends, I agreed to accept the nomination. I might add that it helps in any election to be the only candidate on the slate for the office you seek.

As president of the Educational Secretaries, I saw the need for a stronger voice to speak for us. We were not being heard by the Board; our members were insignificant and our clout non-existent, but I was unwilling to let our independence be swallowed up by the Chicago Teachers Union. I feared the loss of our identity in such a large group of teachers, so when the Union attempted to absorb us into their ranks, our conflict with them began.

Finally the Union called for an election to decide which of our organizations was to be the collective bargaining agent for school clerks. We lost the election because many women preferred the strength of a large Union to what they thought was the ineffectiveness of an independent association. As the victors, the Chicago Teachers Union became the sole collective bargaining agent for us and our association was left without purpose.

After two years' membership in the Chicago Teachers Union, I was eligible to hold office in our Functional Group, so I ran for president. This time I had an opponent who was sponsored by the dominant caucus of the Union. She was a "died in the wool" Union member who believed, "My Union, right or wrong, but my Union." This thinking differed from mine in many ways. By a very slim margin, I was elected head of the School Clerks Functional Group in the Chicago Teachers Union and thus began my career as a Union activist.

Chapter 6
CHICAGO TEACHERS UNION

I do not approve of Unions whose strength overpowers individuals not represented by them; nor do I approve of the exploitation of workers without representation. I did, however, use every opportunity, through the strong voice of the Chicago Teachers Union to address the needs of my school clerks. Much was accomplished for many. School clerks became better workers as their contribution to the public schools became known and recognized. We acquired identities; we no longer were faceless employees imposed upon by our employers. We had a strong voice in our leader, Bob Healey — and the Board no longer was able to manipulate us to their own advantage.

Within the Union we began our uphill climb to justice and dignity. We were a small minority in a big Union and our little voice had to become a big shout before we could be heard. As president of our group, I soon learned how to shout. Some of the women, however, couldn't wait for us to be heard and demanded everything immediately. Living in a world of instant pudding, instant printing and instant annoyances, they had a low tolerance level. I recall an incident, the memory of which has remained with me all these years.

My school clerks were very angry about a change in the formula for school clerk assignments — a change they felt was being ignored by the Union. On my way to a meeting to discuss this with them I wondered how I could placate them before they dragged me out and stoned me to death. Their wrath was intense for such mild-mannered women.

As I paused for a stop light, I saw a handicapped woman clutching a shopping bag and hugging the wall of a building as she walked down the street. The January wind was blustery and cold and every few steps she put her bag down so she could blow on her cold hands. I looked at my warm kid gloves on the seat beside me — the gloves I didn't need in my heated car. The sight of her cold hands moved me to turn back and give her my gloves. As I approached her my heart was moved with compassion. I looked into the ugliest face I had ever seen. There were nostrils, but no nose; there were slits in the eye sockets that were red and unsightly. Her face was scarred and homely. She didn't comprehend my gift of the gloves. She kept pointing to herself, saying, "For me? For me?" — unbelieving but grateful. I said, "Yes, they are for you." As I spoke, I kissed her saying, "God bless you." I believe I touched God in that encounter, for my life since then has taken such radical turns. For many years after that, I passed the same corner daily but I never saw the woman again.

When I returned to my car, sobbing uncontrollably, I knew what I would say to the members at the meeting. Their big gripe decreased in size to nothing. How could anything be so upsetting when God had blessed them so abundantly?

At the meeting I told them about the woman I had met — a woman who, but for the grace of God, could have been any one of us. I asked the school clerks to thank God for their health, and for their appearance that didn't frighten people. Yes, and to thank God also, for the job that, at the present time, aggravated them. I asked them to be patient and accept the good life they had in spite of things that were disturbing to them. They responded beautifully and I believe all our lives were touched by that experience of God among His people.

In 1971 our School Clerks Functional Group set up a fund for the hearing-impaired children in our schools. The fund provides financial assistance for the purchase of hearing aids, and finances the purchase of carpeting needed to deaden the sounds amplified by the pupils' hearing aids. The fund also provides an annual $1,000 scholarship for a student graduating from one of our classes in the Special Education Department. This money is raised from an annual luncheon and Ad Book. The cause is a good one, but the fellowship it engenders is even greater, as school clerks give of their time and their talents to be of service to others who need their help.

A great deal was accomplished through our membership in the Chicago Teachers Union. While I object to the abuse of Union power I will always uphold the need for a strong Union to speak out on behalf of workers who have no defense against ruthless employers who exploit them. Such employers measure their success by their positions of authority rather than by the development of their own God-given talents which enabled them to achieve their goals.

Chapter 7
OUR LADY OF MT. CARMEL
COMMITTEE ON COMMUNITY LIFE

After my years of child-raising, I was left with only one speed and that was FAST. From my empty nest I had to find something to do with my spare time, so when I heard about the formation of a parish committee on community life, it sounded like my answer to be needed by someone, somewhere. It was another stirring of my involved life and I responded to it.

The chairperson of the meeting was a very dedicated young man named Karl Payton. Karl was setting up various sub-committees and enlisting volunteers to chair them. They planned a Liturgy Committee, A Music Ministry, Hospitality Committee, etc. After listening to the plans for all these different sub-committees, I raised my hand and asked if we couldn't have a committee that worked with people. Karl agreed with the need for such a group and asked if I would chair it. It was something I wanted so I said, "Yes, I'll be glad to get something started." That was the origin of the "Person to Person Volunteers." We were just that - wherever there was a need, we were available to provide the service on a one to one basis.

The Committee on Community Life sponsored two annual affairs: a picnic in Lincoln Park and a Thanksgiving Dinner for senior citizens and handicapped. The picnic was a day of fun in the sun for all of us and "it never rained on our parade." The planned agenda included an exciting baseball game between the big and the little kids (adults and children); a barbecue with an ethnic flavor and races and games of interest to all ages. In the frivolity of the afternoon we became better acquainted with our people. Friendships were formed that brought us into each other's homes and personal lives. The rapport established by our volunteers at this outing gave our friends a shoulder to lean on and a friend to count on. The "haves" and the "have nots" became united in satisfying their needs — that need we all have to help or to be helped. God's pattern is so beautiful. It's too bad so many of His children reject it. We are meant to live together in His love, not in the segregation of our strengths and weaknesses.

Our Thanksgiving dinner for seniors and handicapped was another fun day. Some volunteers bought and prepared the food and made all the necessary arrangements for serving the meal; others transported the invited guests from their home to the school hall; others planned the entertainment.

Our guests enjoyed a home-cooked meal served by people who cared about them and in the entertainment and joy of the day, they forgot that they were lonely or forgotten. In the busyness of our lives most of us are oblivious to the boredom of solitude that is the fate of so many formerly active men and women who now are isolated from work and unable to do the things they once enjoyed. I suggest to anyone looking for God that He can be found in the midst of His people living the blessings of the Beatitudes — those teachings that tell us to "Love one another. Such as my love has been for you, so must your love be for each other." (Jn. 13:34)

Chapter 8
PERSON TO PERSON VOLUNTEERS

The Person to Person Volunteers became a viable part of life in Our Lady of Mount Carmel Parish. In our neighborhoods we sometimes overlook many beautiful people, both young and old, who want to be of service. All they need is someone to tap them on the shoulder and ask for their help. So I began my involved life by "shoulder tapping."

Our services were varied, as our animated corps of volunteers ministered to the needs of families, shut-ins and the elderly. Many of our families were Puerto Ricans who were having difficulties adapting to their new lives on the mainland, others were recipients of Public Aid who were being treated as nondescript people. We wanted to help these people to help themselves. Sometimes the children needed tutoring, or were in need of clothing. At other times the parents needed a helping hand from a friend. Our volunteers were always there, not as "do-gooders," but as personal friends to those who needed our friendship.

I had about 20 volunteers who were available 24 hours a day for whatever service might be needed. The elderly were a special concern of our volunteers who became loving grandchildren to many lonely and unloved old people. The assistance given to this group was in the area of transportation to and from Sunday mass, to doctor's appointments and shopping. Apartments were decorated at Christmas time and our volunteers became the elderly's link to the outside world in the letters they wrote for them.

It would be impossible to describe all the work done by the Person to Person Volunteers, so I will just highlight some of the most memorable cases.

Baby-Sitting Service

The Person to Person Volunteers provided baby sitting service for our members attending the Sunday, 11:15 guitar mass. Youngsters who were members of families being helped by us were our baby-sitters. The parents of the little ones who were being cared for, paid a small fee each week to our young sitters who worked under the direction of an adult volunteer.

The program had a dual purpose for it introduced our parents to some very reliable baby-sitters looking for jobs. Again, the simple thing of people helping people.

Hilda

While in a grocery store one day I was approached by a little old lady who inquired of me the price of some item, explaining that she was shopping for a handicapped person who did not have much money and worried about the cost of everything. I told her what she wanted to know, then asked the name and address of the woman to see if I could be of any help to her.

My call on Hilda was an eye opener. She was supposed to have had a broken back, but I learned later that her biggest problem was alcohol. Her arm could have been broken from hoisting so much booze to her lips, but if her back was broken (which I always doubted), I know she didn't break it cleaning her apartment which was a pigsty.

Hilda had emphysema, was as dirty about herself as she was about her home, and was a real manipulator of people. She had been an actress and never lost her ability to perform. All of this, however, did not lessen Hilda's need for help. I thought the most important thing we could give her was a better self-image and an apartment that would reflect that image. The opportunity to go ahead with my plan came when Hilda, in need of round-the-clock oxygen therapy was taken to the hospital. In her absence I called together a "bucket brigade" of PPV, who met at Hilda's for a day of wall washing, rug cleaning, window washing and general renovation of her filthy hovel. The task was a big one, but the camaraderie was fun and the rewards great. It was beautiful to see so many people of all ages serving God in such a way. As we were cleaning up her apartment, the hospital personnel were practically sand-blasting Hilda's scummy body. I had hoped that her new-found cleanliness would motivate her to remain clean, but she had no desire to change her ways. Her number one priority was booze not cleanliness!

The first time I realized I was dealing with an alcoholic was when I called on her and found about a dozen bottles of liquor outside her door. Hilda's story was that it was delivered to her house for her brother who was out of town and unable to accept delivery at his apartment. I also discovered that Hilda was, among other things, a liar. I write all this so that you know the service we render to God through His people does not always come wrapped in a beautiful, attractive box with "Thank you" streamers flying from it. Sometimes God's people are dirty, shiftless, irresponsible individuals; but they still are His people needing our help. In order to serve God as He wants to be served, we must ask Him to fill us with His compassion so that we see through His eyes the beauty of His hurting people.

Many of God's children are suffering from their own addictions, from their own rejection of God, from rejections of family, from their inability to cope, from worry over financial needs, or from the emptiness of their false idols. It doesn't matter what caused their suffering; what does matter is that they need help and with God's love flowing through us, we must give that help.

When the local liquor store refused to deliver any more sparkling spirits to Hilda because of her mounting unpaid bills, she began putting the pressure on me to supply her fix of cheap wine (for medicinal purposes, you understand). I could not encourage this addiction but I felt very sorry for her great need of it.

Eventually Hilda was hospitalized for the last time — her cravings finally stilled in death, and I became a little closer to God because I had met Hilda.

Anne Kelly

A nne Kelly was a little old lady who had no family, and not many friends. Two young women, members of PPV, volunteered to look in on Anne from time to time, shop for her and most of all to be her friends. They loved her and she loved them. One evening when they called on Anne, they found her on the floor of her apartment, unable to get up. When they called me I instructed them to send her in an ambulance to the hospital where I would meet her.

Upon arrival at the hospital emergency room she was examined by the doctor on duty who diagnosed the cause of her black-out as a slight stroke brought on by extremely high blood pressure. He then told her she could return home, but needed to be watched very closely. When I told him she couldn't go home as she lived alone and could not care for herself, the doctor said, ''Lady, if this woman were my own mother, I couldn't find a bed for her in this hospital tonight.'' I replied, ''If she were your mother she wouldn't need a bed because she would have you to take care of her.'' I then added rather angrily, ''It's too bad they don't require doctors to have a heart before they award them their M.D.'s.'' After about an hour, the doctor returned, still infuriated over my accusation and said, ''We'll keep Miss Kelly in the hall tonight and find a room for her in the morning.'' He then added, in retaliation, ''And don't you tell me I don't have a heart.'' To which I replied, ''I knew you did, that's why I said what I did.''

Anne remained in the hospital for about three weeks when she was transferred to a nursing home. She died about a year later after having been placed in about three different homes. The pastor of Our Lady of Mt. Carmel provided Anne with a beautiful burial service attended by mourners and pall bearers recruited from our PPV and Women's Club. Father Byrne's homily was a beautiful tribute to a little old lady who had nothing in life, but had the glory of a real resurrection at her funeral mass. Anne would have loved it for her only request had been for a Catholic burial.

Marion Gumm

Marion Gumm was a very proud woman, paralyzed and blind, who had retired from County Hospital where she had been a nurse for many years. Like so many others, she didn't like to admit that she needed help. Too often our society stigmatizes those who need help, even though circumstances beyond their control might have brought about their limitations. Marion's pension was pre-inflationary and very minimal.

Two young girls, members of a Puerto Rican family we were helping, offered to assist Marion. They went to her apartment every day, cleaned her rooms, did her shopping, took care of her mail, opened cans of food for her meals, and set out everything else she needed. Because of Marion's pride, she insisted on giving each child a quarter for her help, never understanding that the greatest compensation for these youngsters was the joy they found in helping someone who needed them as they needed us.

One evening, about 11:00 p.m. Marion called to say that she had fallen and was unable to get up from the floor without the help of the police who were at her apartment. The police wanted to take her to the nearest hospital, but Marion wanted to go to the hospital where her doctor was a staff member. She wanted me to plead her case to the policemen. They have their rules though and they could not take her to a more distant hospital. I called Jerry Reedy, one of our volunteers, and asked him to meet me at Marion's so we could take her to the hospital of her choice. Jerry wheeled Marion from her apartment, carried her down a flight of stairs and put her in my car. This was no easy task, as Marion wore a heavy brace and was paralyzed on her left side. We took her to the hospital where the two of us, as next of kin, signed her in as a patient. We remained with her until her tests were over and she was happily placed in a room in her doctor's hospital.

During her three weeks stay there, Jerry, his wife, Susan, and their little girls made regular visits to see her. Susan was one of our volunteers who had been a very kind and loving friend of Marion's. The night before Marion was to be transferred to a nursing home, she died, while prayers were being said for her by the Person to Person Volunteers who had become her family.

Mercy Nuns Infirmary

Thousands of people passed the Mercy Infirmary on busy Belmont Avenue every day giving no thought to the loneliness of the elderly and sick nuns who resided there; women who had given their lives in service to God through their work with the children of Chicago. Could we not take the time to pause, go inside and say, "Thank you, Sister. You taught my children many years ago at such and such a school?" We did not mean to hurt or neglect them but the priorities of the present often obscure the past and we forget to express the gratitude we feel.

Our PPV were concerned about what these nuns, who were no longer able to work had once meant to us. Without hesitation we decided to adopt the Infirmary as one of our ministries. I contacted Sister Innocentia, the sister in charge, and asked her to help set up a schedule for our volunteers. With Sister's concern for her charges and our reaching out to them, a significant change was manifested in their lives. Some of our volunteers would read to the sisters, others would write notes for them, still others would stop by just to say "Hi" or to take them for a walk around the neighborhood. Sister Innocentia made us comfortable in the sharing of our lives. She was like a mother to her sick and elderly nuns, many of whom were much younger than she.

During the holidays a car pool was set up to drive the sisters through the city to view the beautiful Christmas decorations. Our tour was preceded by a nice dinner at their choice of restaurants which was a pancake house. We selected the restaurant once by taking them to the beautiful Martinique on the south side of Chicago where we celebrated the 92nd birthday of one of the nuns. At the table next to us was a gentleman who had been taught by our birthday girl. He bought us a round of champagne with which we toasted our honored guest while enjoying an evening of celebrating and reminiscing.

When the sisters moved from the Infirmary to Mercy Manor in Aurora, the PPV followed them and continued our annual drive and restaurant treat. In the Fall of the year, about eight volunteers drove to Aurora, Illinois for the outing. As each driver arrived at the Manor, they were warmly greeted by the nuns, who were like children anxiously awaiting the start of a great adventure. The child-like joy reflected in the faces of these women was a delight to see and once again I was reminded of how little God's people need to make them happy for they have within themselves that inner joy and peace that comes from walking with the Lord.

When all the volunteers arrived from Chicago and passengers were assigned to their cars, we drove to the Ponderosa Steak House in Naperville where we enjoyed a tasty lunch and the camaraderie of our friends. We then returned to our cars for a drive through the Morton Arboretum, a botanical garden exhibiting a natural setting of trees and flowers. God was in charge of entertainment that day and He provided a country-side ablaze with the panorama of Mother Nature's indescribable beauty. The "Ohs"! and "Ahs"! of our friends as they viewed the colorful splendor were God's "Thank you" to us. It was fun being used by Him to bring such joy to His children. The pleasure of the day was far-reaching as the sisters anticipated the afternoon outing for weeks beforehand and relived the fun of it in their memories for weeks afterwards. They thanked us over and over again, and promised to remember us in their prayers. I know that such a powerhouse of prayers and prayers has, and will continue to enrich my life.

Jose and Marita

One incident that always will stand out in my memory is one in which Divine Providence really out-did Himself. "For man it is impossible; but for God all things are possible." (Matt.19:26)

One of our parish priests called to tell me of a young family in need of help from our volunteers. I called on the mother who could speak no English. She took me to her sister-in-law, who interpreted for me the needs of this family.

Both parents had been working to support themselves and their two-year-old son, but Marita, the mother, was now seven months pregnant and her employer had terminated her employment. The little boy was sleeping with his parents for want of his own bed, and they had no clothes or crib for the infant they were expecting. They had no money saved as their combined income was minimal. Both parents were very young high school drop-outs. The hospital had refused to accept Marita as a pre-natal patient without an advance deposit on her confinement. Our assignment was monumental. I assured Marita that I didn't know what I could do for her, but I knew someone who did have the answers, and that was the Holy Spirit. I told her I'd be in touch with Him and later, with her.

Upon returning to my apartment and, after a little prayer for guidance, I called a maintenance man in one of the high-rise buildings along the lake front. He had been very cooperative in the past in giving us furniture, clothing, etc., that had been left behind by tenants. When I told him what I needed he was flabbergasted as he replied, "Just today I had a tenant move and leave behind a beautiful white crib with a spotless mattress. They also left behind a matching youth bed. Could you use that too, along with two chests of drawers?" It was my turn to be speechless, but by now I had become accustomed to the surprises of the Holy Spirit, so I just said, "Great, I can use everything. I'll pick it up tomorrow, but I'll call you before I come." At that time I had on hand a beautiful layette which had been ordered from the Christ Child Association as a Christmas gift for an infant whose parents had moved out of the parish and left no forwarding address.

A phone call to Joan Slack and Dolores Butterfield, two of my dependable volunteers, provided me with a van and woman-power to pick up the furniture. Upon the delivery of the furniture and layette, Marita and her husband looked at me as if I were a magician. I just said, "I told you I didn't know what help I could get for you, but I knew someone who did. The gifts you have received are truly God's gifts to you. We are just delivering them. Thank God, not us."

Arrangements for Marita's confinement and prenatal care were also confirmed when the PPV gave the hospital the deposit they required. How beautifully God takes care of His people who trust in Him!

Bob and Mildred Indolence

"Hello, Rosemary? This is Father Goodwill. I need a little help for a disabled couple. Could you get someone to take them to the laundromat every week? They live over a tavern on Halsted and need a ride to the laundromat." Because we were able to meet the needs of all who called on us, I just said, "I'm sure I can, Father. Could I have their name and address?"

Upon visiting the couple to determine the extent of the assistance they needed, I learned that they really didn't need anyone to TAKE them to the laundromat — what they wanted was someone to BE their laundromat and do their washing FOR them every week. The husband was ambulatory, though on crutches, and the wife was very able-bodied, but psychotic. Rather than a laundress, I would have prescribed a touch of ambition for Pa and a psychiatrist for Ma, but in their own minds they were convinced they needed help. So. . . . . . help they got. Not wanting to tie down any volunteer to this weekly chore, I took the job myself.

Once a week I'd go to their apartment, pick up their soiled clothes, take the bag of laundry to my building where I would wash, dry and fold the clean clothes. One day when I was returning the finished laundry, I was introduced to their teenage grandson who was visiting them from one of our nearby suburbs. In the bedroom was his young mother (probably in her early thirties) taking a nap. At this time, I was in my sixties, and after working all day was returning the wash I had done the night before. The thoughts that went through my mind cannot be printed. In fact, I still ask God's forgiveness for having had such thoughts.

I cried out to God, "Why do you expect an old lady like me to wait on people like this when they could have their own daughter do the work that is needed to be done? She's much younger and more able than I am." God really answered me that day. He seemed to say, "You asked to be my instrument. Isn't the use of an instrument determined by the user, not by the instrument? Perhaps I want to use you to teach that selfish young daughter to assume her responsibility in caring for her parents. My child, don't try to understand my ways, let me use you as I wish to bring others to my Father's house." It might have been my imagination speaking to me, but I was satisfied with the answer and continued my weekly visits until the family moved out of our area.

My Creator's plan, while beyond my understanding, is not beyond my accepting.

Toys for Our Little Friends

Sister Ludivine is a Parish Visitor of Mary Immaculate. She was sent to Our Lady of Mount Carmel to take the census, but her involvement in the life of the parish finally resulted in the census taking becoming her secondary assignment. She was a key person in our PPV activities and most of our referrals came from her. After telling us about the need of some parishioner, she would refer it to the Holy Spirit who worked with us in finding solutions. Sounds like a peculiar approach to problem solving, but there was no question in my mind that the answers could only have come from above.

One Christmas, Father Ferrigan, our parish priest, received a large donation of new toys for the needy children in our parish. Since most of these children were known to us, Sister Ludivine and I were asked to distribute them. We packed the trunk of my car and off we went on one of the fun trips of my life. We gave the toys to the parents so they could be Santa Claus to their children. It was more important that the gifts came from them for we were just the under-cover distributors.

On one of our deliveries I was waiting for Sister to return to the car after taking some toys into a home. The trunk of my car was still open, displaying all the shiny new toys, when a little boy passed by with his grandmother. He stopped and stared wistfully at the toys. When I offered him his choice his grandmother glanced at me to be sure I meant what I said. The little lad then reached into the trunk, took out a big red fire truck and walked away with a smile and a "Thanks" that told the world he had found Santa Claus and it wasn't even Christmas. I felt ten feet tall and thanked God for giving me the opportunity to bring such joy to a little child.

Chapter 9

AMERICAN RED CROSS

A few years after I began driving for the Apostolate of the Handicapped, my six year old Buick started getting tired and troublesome. I knew I could continue to drive the car, but I doubted the old gal's reliability in transporting handicapped persons. I could walk away from a stalled car, my disabled could not.

At that time someone told me about an appeal being made by the American Red Cross for volunteer drivers. Upon investigation I learned that as a volunteer driver, a station wagon would be available to me for transporting the handicapped each month. So I signed up as a Red Cross volunteer driver and a new area of service opened up to me. Once again I met many beautiful people among the volunteers and those we served.

As a driver, my services varied from taking the elderly to doctors' appointments, taking a blind veteran to the bus station and returning him to the Vets' hospital after his weekend at home, taking patients to outings from nursing homes and/or half-way houses, to picking up eyes (yes, EYES) from the airport or from the Illinois Eye and Ear Hospital, for delivery to hospitals where doctors would implant the cornea in a patient hoping that such a transplant would restore vision.

The service involving the transporting of human eyes was the hardest to explain to the squeamish people who thought only of the eye in the case I carried. I thought of the wonders of God's creatures who had developed procedures in which doctors could restore sight to the sightless. Many thoughts come to mind when I think of the eye pick-ups from the airport. The box is vividly marked "HUMAN EYES, HANDLE WITH CARE." I enjoyed watching the reactions of the people I passed. Some were really frightened (as if the poor eye could hurt them), others were amused, others wondered if it was a gag and I am sure there were many who thought as I did — "What a beautiful gift from God."

I remember once placing the container in my refrigerator at home where I stopped after a pick-up at the airport. On that day, my granddaughter, Pat, came over to visit. She opened the refrigerator to get something and upon seeing the box marked "HUMAN EYES" she almost went into shock as she excitedly called out to me, "Gram, do you know what's in the Fridge?" She wasn't at the house when I had come from the airport so I really had forgotten about the box of eyes. I just said, "Of course I know. There's food in there, what else?" All the while I was thinking it was some kind of a joke. "No, Gram I mean that box marked HUMAN EYES. Are there really eyes in that box"? Knowing how disturbed she was I thought I'd have a little fun with her. "Yes, there are eyes in the box — the most beautiful blue eyes you have ever seen." I was going pretty far, for we never opened the sealed box and to this day, I have no idea what the cornea, the eye or whatever I picked up looked like. I went on to tell her that the eyes wouldn't hurt her, that they couldn't even see her, but I was unsuccessful in dispelling her fears.

I loved this particular service as I would visualize through my mind's eye the joy that would come to one human because of the compassionate generosity of another. I never had the car radio on when I was transporting eyes, for I prayed constantly while driving and I thanked God for allowing me to contribute my little part to the greatness of His work. I asked God to bless the recipient whose sight would be restored, and to keep that person always aware of His great gift.

I remember the first time that I drove the Red Cross van. I went to the office to pick up my assignment and was given the keys to a van which I had never driven. I told the man that I wasn't sure I could drive it. He said, "Take it around the block and get the feel of it. The number of people you are picking up will not fit in a station wagon, so you'll have to use the van." My assignment was to pick up 12 people from a nursing home and take them to a performance at the Masonic Temple in Chicago. So I drove around the block, felt a little nervous, but returned and told the dispatcher that I'd try to handle the van for the afternoon. I was given a challenge — conquer your fear or disappoint those lonely people. You can be sure I got rid of my fear. On the way to pick up my passengers, I drove on Lake Shore Drive along the lake where a gusty wind kept nudging the van, causing it to sway black and forth. I felt like I was steering a sailboat in a tornado, so on the trip back to the temple with my passengers, I took the city streets where the wind lost its power to intimidate me. I believe my successful confrontation with the blustery winds gave me confidence to drive like a veteran cabby the rest of the day.

I like to repeat what one of my first Saturday passengers told the doorman in his building. "If you see a Red Cross station wagon pull into the drive without a driver, don't be frightened — it'll be Rosemary coming to pick me up. She's there even if you can't see her."

I still am a volunteer driver for the Red Cross and even though I continue to become involved in new and different causes, I hate to let go of any of my services; they are to me what recreation is to others.

Chapter10
CHARISMATIC RENEWAL

Sister Ludivine had a key to my apartment which she used as a resting place while covering her beat — our parish community. Many afternoons, upon my return from work I'd find her relaxing there and it was on these occasions that we'd get into discussions about the Charismatic Renewal which had transformed her life so completely. She persisted in her invitations to Helen McSloy and me to attend a prayer meeting with her saying, "Try it. I know you'll like it." But we were adamant in our "No, thanks." I thought I was a good Catholic who knew God and loved Him so I just said, "I like my church the way it is. I don't need all that Charismatic hoop-la. You go and have your fun, but count me out."

One day after Sister had been transferred to New York and had stopped bugging us, our curiosity got the better of us and Helen and I decided to look in on a prayer meeting. I must admit we found it very weird, snickered a little about the raising of hands and the strange tongues, but the warmth and love generated in the group was something we wanted to experience again. Until that first prayer meeting I was unaware of God's time table. Everything unusual that had happened prior to then had been accepted as strange coincidences — now I was beginning to see God's hand in the implementation of His laws.

At our first prayer meeting I viewed with great apprehension the "praying over" individuals who asked for special prayer support. I was too sophisticated for that sort of thing — but to each his own, and as one of the group, I, too, prayed over those requesting prayers. In my arrogance though, I felt myself too intelligent for such a demonstrative expression of prayer. This was shortly after Vatican II when all the changes seemed superfluous to us old timers. Our church was beautiful in its solemnity and its splendor and needed nothing added to or subtracted from it.

On the Sunday following our first prayer meeting I had a birthday party at my apartment for my brother, Bill. When the party ended at about 10:00 p.m. the guests left for home and at 11:30 that night I received a call from Wesley Memorial Hospital telling me that Bill was in their emergency room after having been severely beaten and mugged by six young thugs. The assault had taken place in the parking lot behind Fourth Presbyterian Church on Michigan Avenue, within a few feet of the entrance to my brother's apartment. My notification of the attack came from the pastor of the church. He was the Good Samaritan who found Bill unconscious and had the time and compassion to take him to the hospital and notify the family whose names were in Bill's wallet.

With prayers on my lips, compassion in my heart and eyes filled with tears, I left for the hospital. My sister and brother-in-law were already there and together we were taken to the intensive care unit where Bill was being treated. It was difficult for me to believe that the person I was looking at was my brother, for I had seen him just a few hours before, alive and vibrant in the joyful celebration of his birthday. The doctor explained to us the extent of his injuries. He had three broken ribs, a fractured jaw, a slight skull fracture and head lacerations which required 30 stitches. My heart ached for him. He looked so beaten, so tired, and so battered that I cried for him and for the cruelty of man's inhumanity to man. All the attackers were black, and Bill was a white teacher of mentally handicapped youngsters in an all black school. I prayed that the incident would not embitter him. I needn't have worried. As soon as he was able to speak he assured me that it would not alter his love for his students. "If they were with me," he said, "They would have defended me." He didn't blame the black people for the viciousness of the crime. He blamed the individuals who happened to be black, and in no way did it affect his feelings for his staff, his students or their parents. I can't tell you how proud I was of Bill.

The following day, Helen and I attended our second prayer meeting at which I told them of the incident and our need for prayers. Without hesitation they sat me on a chair in the middle of the group, laid hands on me and on each other as they prayed and chanted in tongues, praising God and beseeching His mercy and healing for Bill. I had just met these people the week before and I was overwhelmed by the warmth of their love and deep concern. Their solemn petitions seemed to go up like incense directly to our God. I felt great power in the prayers of these simple people who boldly professed their faith and love incomplete abandonment of self. They were simple only in their deep faith and trust in God, for among them were several priests and nuns, doctors, lawyers, teachers and other professionals. I was baptized a Catholic in 1912, but found the Spirit of my Living God in 1970 in the Charismatic Renewal.

On Tuesday I visited my brother and noticing that his jaw was not wired as the doctor had ordered, I asked Bill about it. He said, "They must have made a mistake in reading the X-rays because the jaw isn't broken." The nurse explained the phenomenon by saying, "We know that bones don't move so the X-ray plate must have." I wished I had been there to respond, "Who says so?" I then asked Bill if the ribs were painful, for I saw him moving about very comfortably. He said, "They aren't going to tape the ribs either, because they have concluded that the ribs were bruised, not broken." WOW! I could hardly wait to witness to God's healing power in the erroneously read X-rays and the bruised, rather than broken ribs. I couldn't contain my excitement so I told him about the prayer meeting and all the prayers said for him; giving all credit to the prayers of the Charismatics. He accepted the prayers with thanks, but added, "Don't forget, I've been storming heaven myself. Don't discount my prayers." My brother is a super conservative Catholic. He tolerated my enthusiasm for the Renewal but rejected it for himself. That experience of faith and healing created in me a thirst for the word of God and the fellowship of extroverted Christians, so Helen and I attended one meeting after another until we had become addicted to the Charismatic Renewal. I wondered why I had waited so long to discover all that my Lord wanted to give me. As the old German saying goes, "Ve get so soon aldt, und so late schmart!"

On the day I received the Baptism of the Holy Spirit, I felt as though God came down from heaven just to be with me. I felt like the men from Emmaus who said, "Were not our hearts burning inside us as he talked to us on the road and explained the scriptures to us?" (Luke 24:32) My heart has been on fire ever since that day and I hear those words, "Follow Me" as clearly as His disciples must have heard them, and I humbly ask the Holy Spirit to guide and direct me in the ways of my Heavenly Father.

Among those introduced to me by Sister Ludivine in our parish work was a charming woman named Veronica Hill who had been an alcoholic for more than thirty years. When Sister left Chicago she asked me to do what I could to help Veronica, for she knew she would need and respond to anyone reaching out to her. Veronica had known all the despair and hopelessness associated with her addiction, but there was a charm about her that made people want to help her.

I introduced Veronica to the Charismatic prayer meetings and went through the Life in the Spirit Seminar with her. At her Baptism in the Holy Spirit, Veronica received a healing from her alcoholism — but even more than that she grew in her love of God as Mary Magdalene must have when she met Jesus. As much was forgiven both women, their gratitude was in proportion to their grace of forgiveness. It is now more than 14 years since Veronica's healing and many lives have been blessed by their encounters with her and her deep faith and love of God.

In the Charismatic Renewal I found love without compromise, help without begging, forgiveness without penalty. I found all this because I found my living God; the One who had been hidden, but worshipped and adored by me throughout my life. I found the greatness of a Creator who wants to walk with those He created. I found a love that cannot be documented, but can call forth faith that moves mountains — mountains of frustrations, fears and anxieties, mountains that are not of Him, and mountains that are the attachments to the things of the world. His love levels all these mountains when our walk through life is with our hand in His.

I had already begun my life of involvement with my co-workers, my parish, the handicapped and the American Red Cross, but before the Charismatic Renewal, I thought it was my work being done for Him, now I know it was His work being done through me. I finally have allowed myself to become one of God's puppets — not a mindless, hollow toy on a string, but a real, live human puppet who had learned to let the teachings of Christ permeate my life and dominate my actions. I pray to Him and thank Him for His answers, whether those answers are negative or affirmative, for I have learned to live in His Holy Will, trusting Him for all that I need. Struggles and sufferings are tools by which God calls us to Himself. They are the rungs of the ladder we must climb to reach our eternal reward. Even molded clay is of no use until it is fired; how much more do we need the fire of God's love to mold us into His likeness — that likeness that will change the cross we carry into the crown we wear.

In 1975 I flew to Rome with 200 Christians to attend the International Charismatic Conference. Oh, such grandeur! such solemnity! as we entered St. Peter's with all of us singing our "Alleluias" to the Lord. The memory of that conference calls me to an inner quiet and profound relationship with my God. I think my great awareness of His presence was awakened in me at that time. Learning the precepts of my faith was important, but more important is the joy I have found in living in His presence. Spirit-filled people, sharing their faith in the diversity of an international gathering, leveled us all to the simplicity of being God's children gathered together to worship and adore Him as we frolicked in His love.

Chapter 11
LOYOLA-MUNDELEIN INTERCESSORY PRAYER GROUP

A fter receiving the Baptism of the Holy Spirit, I wanted to share my joy and my love of the Lord with everyone, particularly with my handicapped friends who were unable to attend prayer meetings because of architectural barriers or lack of transportation. In the brokenness of their bodies and the desolation of their limited lives, they needed to live in the presence of a God who was their personal Savior.

Because my cross had been made light through my involvement in the Charismatic Renewal, I wanted to share this new-found joy and peace with my dear friends. Their handicaps had not made saints of them, but God was calling them to accept their disabilities in His name and to let His love shine through their handicap. He needs their witness before a materialistic world that ignores the redemptive suffering of the cross.

With the help of Sister Marina Kennelly, the foundress of my Loyola-Mundelein Prayer Group, I organized the Loyola-Mundelein Prayer Group for Handicapped. Our first meetings were held at St. Malachy's Church where Sister Maude McGreal had interceded with her pastor for the use of his church. Since people do not readily accept new beginnings we initially attracted only 12 men and women — half of whom were handicapped. When our credibility became established many others wanted to join us so we began looking for a new location which would be more accessible to the severely handicapped.

Once again, at the request of two Sacred Heart nuns, Sisters Mary Munch and Verona Denkman, we were granted the use of the gym at Sacred Heart Academy which was ideally located and totally accessible. Soon our prayer group of 12 was increased to 30 disabled persons and approximately 15 drivers and helpers. What fellowship and joy we experienced as we praised our God in song and prayer for, "Where two or three are gathered in my name, there am I in their midst." (Mt.18:20) He was truly with us.

Through our Intercessory prayer meetings, I have enjoyed the friendship of many beautiful people — some seemingly forgotten ones who have few worldly goods, but have that peace and contentment which is the presence of God's love in their lives.

These special people now enjoy a closer walk with God because of our prayer meetings; but their intercession for us on behalf of all the particular needs of our society is blessing our church, our city and our world. Our special prayer petitions are for priests and religious and for all the families and young adults of our city who are struggling to find God in the confusion of their lives.

Chapter 12

I BEGIN TO DREAM

As I looked forward to retirement, thoughts began to bounce around in my mind as to how I would be spending those years. My life had been a busy one, first with my own family responsibilities and now with my involvement in other people's lives. How would I handle inactivity and dependency? I had heard that many people dry up like prunes after they retired. I don't even like to eat prunes — and I certainly never wanted to look like one. My nest-egg wasn't large, I didn't like traveling and I was sure a great deal of my pension check would be needed to keep the tarnish off my "golden years." The visions that danced in my head were not of sugar plums as in *The Night Before Christmas*. No the visions that danced in my head were mean and ugly little thoughts of deteriorating health, waning energy, dimmed vision and failing memory. What dismal thoughts. All those attributes which had enabled me to successfully pursue my goals would be diminishing in my retirement. There was only one part of me that was becoming better as I grew older, and that one thing, for me, was the essential ingredient for a happy life, my awareness of God's love for me. My love for Him had grown throughout the years — first out of my desperate need of someone to love and understand me, then in thanksgiving to Him for enriching my life by His use of me to do His work. Would that change in retirement? I thought not.

So I began to dream dreams. Dreams of living more fully in His love. How does one do that when senility starts setting in? One does that by ignoring the possible horrors of the future and living in the joy of the present, using each talent to the fullest and uniting each suffering with the suffering of our Savior. I had found my past happiness in God's love; that love which had been given or received as circumstances demanded. The interchange of that love united me with many beautiful people. I reviewed the many facets of my past, knowing that one of them would have to be pursued into my retirement years. Which one, then could I take into the future with me?

Because I had been so intimately involved with the handicapped, there was one particular area of need that I thought had never been met. That need was supportive family services for persons without families of their own. More than once I saw handicapped persons, young and old, placed in state institutions or nursing homes when those caring for them were no longer available to them. I began to think of how I might help these people by sharing my life with them in some manner. What about a Christian community where physically handicapped might live together as a family, helping one another? People who couldn't live alone, would still be able to live independently if an extended family were available to them. I didn't know for sure if this was possible, but I prayed to the Holy Spirit for guidance and the more I prayed the more convinced I became that this was going to be my third career. Retirement, yes, but not one free from responsibilities. I could continue to live out my life being needed by someone.

One day, while thinking that I might be on an ego trip of some kind, I asked God to confirm my plans. Were these His plans as I thought they were — or were they my own foolish ideas? If the plans were His, I prayed that He confirm them with a verse from Scripture. I opened the Bible at random to Joshua 1:5, "No one can withstand you while you live. I will be with you as I was with Moses: I will not leave you nor forsake you." and Joshua 1:9 "I command you: Be firm and steadfast! Do not fear nor be dismayed, for the Lord your God, is with you wherever you go."

I was humbled by the nearness of God in His response to my

prayer. His words spoke so clearly to me, that all my doubts were dispelled. I knew what I was going to do and I prayed for divine guidance and direction to accomplish the work He called me to do. I can't explain the certainty I felt about my future. God was calling me, an old lady with no money, no prestige and no degrees, to establish a home where His special children, the handicapped, could reflect His love in their lives and live abundantly in His Divine Providence. A big, big assignment for one thinking of all those deteriorations of mind and body. However, the words of Isaiah 40:31 came to mind, "They that hope in the Lord will renew their strength, they will soar as with eagles' wings; they will run and not grow weary, walk and not grow faint. " I would trust and wait on the Lord.

Chapter 13
SEED MONEY FOR A DREAM

I was so excited about my plans for the future that I felt I HAD to talk to someone about it or explode! Pam Green, a 21-year old friend of mine was one of those I told about my dream. Pam is a very out-going and loving young southern Miss who had adopted Helen McSloy and me as her surrogate mothers. Her own mother lived in Baton Rouge. My plans were certain, but the execution of them was still in the dream stage. Pam, however, with the impatience of youth, decided some action should be taken. She wanted to push my secret out of the closet into Our Lady of Mt.Carmel parish hall where she planned a fund-raising dinner to provide seed money for my dream.

The dinner wasn't a surprise to me although it started out as such. One day Helen told Pam, "I think you should tell Rosemary. You know she'll hear about it from someone else and it will sound a lot more appealing if you're the one to tell her." Pam accepted the suggestion saying, "O.K. if you think so, but I'm not going to let her talk me out of it." My reputation often preceded me, and wasn't always my best recommendation. At any rate, Pam told me of her plans with the admonition —— "And don't try to stop me!" I knew then that my dream was coming out of hibernation and would awaken in OLMC parish hall the night of the dinner. My walk in faith was exciting to me even though I didn't understand the certainty I felt about the home I wanted to establish. I didn't know where or when, but I was sure it would be opened someday, somewhere, and it would be a real witness to the power of God's love which enabled me to turn my life over to Him without reservation. I was His and He was mine!

I gave God total responsibility for the inspiration of the dream; I would also give Him praise and thanksgiving for the realization of it and finally I'd give Him thanks for the success of its fulfillment. That left me free to do the nitty-gritty things that were within my limited ability, but the heavy stuff I referred to Him. In planning for this fund-raiser, Pam used the same rationale. She had the ability to put it together, but she knew that God Himself would be the unseen chairperson.

After all the preliminary plans were formalized and permission obtained from Father Healy for use of the hall, Pam called together the Committee on Community Life to make arrangements for the dinner. She recruited the parents of the children for whom I sat on Sundays, for the actual planning and preparation of the meal. To others, she gave the responsibility for the publicity and printing of tickets; to others, she gave the responsibility of decorating the hall and the planning of the program; while still others were to arrange transportation for the handicapped. Food donations were received from merchants in the area, and the members of CCL worked together to be part of the dream that God had given me. He called them all to respond to the enthusiasm of His word: "It is God, for His own loving purpose, who puts both the will and the action into you." (Phil 2:13)

So it was that on a fine day in September, a fund-raising Spaghetti Dinner was served to more than 500 persons. The net proceeds were $1,823 which provided me with funds to begin my paper work for the formation of God's Home for His Handicapped. The Person to Person Volunteers had already learned to respond to the needs of people so they were a "natural" to respond to this need.

The magnetism of God's call was manifested to me in that gathering — many of whom thought they were there because they believed in the cause, not realizing that their compassionate response was a gift from above. There are many who never recognize the hand of God in their lives, even though they respond to Him in the love they feel for His forgotten ones. Our concern for the needs of others reflects the presence of God in our lives and Divine Providence is the action of God in our lives. His people who trust in Him!

THE HOLY SPIRIT LED ME TO THE SHELTER OF GOD'S LOVE

My Love Life .... Part Three

Chapter 1
A DREAM UNFOLDS

To be old and to be challenged - how exciting! In setting up a new way of life for the physically handicapped, I discovered how little I knew about procedures. Like a child I was constantly reaching out for people to help me find my way through the maze of paper work, rules and regulations. Little did I realize the complications in such a simple little dream. New adventures call for risks, patience, wisdom (mostly other people's) and a lot of footwork. Oh, well what did I expect? I had a leader who had all the answers — I just had to be available to follow orders. My dream was certainly worthwhile, so let it be difficult. Someday it will be a beautiful life for the disabled.

In considering a name for my Home, there was one word that kept going through my mind. That word was "Love." I had been the recipient of love from my family, friends, and co-workers. I knew I had not lived my life as an independent human being. I had leaned on many people, and in my dependence on them, I found the reflection of God's love flowing through them to me. This reflection was the light that brightened the darkness of my life. What did this mean? Aren't there many kind and considerate individuals who deny the existence of God? The love I was receiving could have been a very human reaction. No, I thought to myself. No one could give the kind of unconditional love that I had received unless it came from above. We are made to help one another, but we cannot do that without any thought of reward or self-gratification, unless the love of God has touched us. I was unable to repay the ones who did so much for me, so they didn't get any visible feedback or reward from me. Their act of giving was repaid by the abundance of God's love which had made them the compassionate loving people that they were.

The dictionary has many definitions of love. One of which is "The benevolence and mercifulness of God toward man." This seemed to be what my home was going to reflect in the lives of its residents. It was the benevolence of God that inspired me to share my life with His handicapped. "Them I will bring to my holy mountain and make joyful in my house of prayer." (Isaiah 56:7)

I knew the word "love" had to be a part of the name and since a home is a shelter from the fury of the elements — the words seemed to come together. I thought of God's love as a shelter or protection from the hurts and disappointments of life. The lives of my handicapped would have greater meaning as they gathered together in a Christian community witnessing to the power of God's love in their lives. Our Home would be a beacon of hope for the hopeless and an instrument of a Father's love for those who sought Him in the trials and loneliness of their lives.

Putting my thoughts together, and I'm sure inspired by the Holy Spirit, our Home became the Shelter of God's Love.

One of the first things I had to do was to stake my claim to that name. I inquired from different sources as to how to go about this. I was directed to an office in the State of Illinois Building where I met the man in charge, and gave him a written request for the name, "Shelter of God's Love." At that time a fee of $15.00 was required to do a search to make sure the name was not in use. He read the application then glancing up at me, said, "Shelter of God's Love?" I replied, "Yes, that's the name we want." He looked at me with an expression that I was going to see quite frequently in the months ahead. The look was silent, but the message was clear, "You're a nice old lady — a little off the wall — but humoring you won't hurt me." He then said, "I'm going to start you off by saving you $15.00. I'm sure that name has never been used before. It's yours without the usual search or fee."

I accepted his kindness with a "Thank you, Sir. I appreciate your consideration." When I stepped outside, I said to myself (knowing God would overhear me), "Thanks, God. Now where do I go?" I kept in touch with my Leader for He knew more people than I did and knew the ones who could help me.

Next step was my charter.

Chapter 2

OUR CHARTER

In order to open our proposed home in the State of Illinois a charter was needed. So — another door was opened for me as "someone" learned about my desire as well as my ignorance in establishing a home for the handicapped. That "someone" referred me to the Executive Service Corps of Chicago, where a group of retired professionals volunteer their services in helping individuals with the details of organizing and/or operating a new service venture. I was told to write up a description of my future Home and present it to the Corps for their consideration.

At this office I met Joanne Rasmussen, a woman who sensed my need and my sincerity. She looked over the material I gave her and without any hesitation told me that the first thing I would need in order to obtain a charter was a Board of Directors. "After you select your Board," she said, "a constitution and bylaws must be drawn up by them." Joanne was one of two people (both women) who didn't give me THAT look. Maybe we women understand one another in a way that is not comprehensible to the opposite sex. I was pleased with her approval of our program and grateful for her follow-through in working with us until we obtained our charter.

Following her instructions, I began seeking out people to serve on my Board. Most of those selected were from the Committee on Community Life. I had known and worked with these men and women long enough to know that our home for the handicapped would be of great interest to them. They were compassionate people who were intelligent and hard working. That combination guarantees success. Once the Board was organized, the work on the constitution and bylaws began.

Finally when all necessary information was gathered I took it to a gentleman in the State of Illinois Building for processing. Within a month our application for a charter was accepted and approved. On January 20, 1978 the Shelter of God's Love was incorporated as a not-for-profit organization.

Once again, everything fell into place in a most unusual way. God's stamp of approval was on the work He wanted done, and my efforts were successful.

Chapter 3

BEGINNING AGAIN IN RETIREMENT

After my ideas for the future were made public and confirmed for me in Joshua 1, I began making plans for my retirement. There would be no room in my new life for the things that I had cherished up until now, and I had lost interest in everything except my new goals. Since every beginning must start where something else ends, I took the first bold step toward fulfilling my dream by not renewing the lease on my beautiful apartment. A lease would deny me the freedom of moving as the Spirit led me. The Holy Spirit was a real mover and shaker in my life and I wanted to be free to follow Him.

In preparation for the move on May 1, I began separating myself emotionally and physically from the life I had been living. Attachments to persons or things, along with the desire for a comfortable and secure life were no longer of any interest to me. I felt, I think, like our forefathers must have felt, as they opened new frontiers in our country. They endured many hardships, but by keeping their eyes on the dream of a better life in the new world, they built a mighty nation. My goals weren't much different from those of the early settlers. I wanted to build a better life in God's world for the handicapped, those children of His who already knew the serenity of living in His Holy Will, but lacked the opportunity to publicly reflect that peace to others. I wanted people to know the power and strength of God's love even in the brokenness of our bodies. The goal I set before me was one of witnessing to the greatness of our God through the littleness of His forgotten ones. I knew the Holy Spirit would guide me, and the home that I wanted to open would be His, not mine. The future was exciting!

During a lifetime, people collect many beautiful possessions and I was no different from anyone else. I had accumulated Dresden china dishes, gold glassware, sterling silver place settings and many other lovely things, some of which I had inherited from my parents. I gave something of value to each of my children and then allowed them to take anything else they wanted that I wouldn't need for my Home. In return, I asked them to donate whatever cash they could to my dream. All the furniture that was being placed in storage would become the property of the home for the handicapped, so I wanted my family to have anything that had any sentimental value for them. What they didn't want I sold and literally moved out of my apartment with only the clothes and other necessities I would need during my vagabond days. Everything else was put in storage on a month to month basis. At that time I thought the Lord would move a lot faster than He did. A nun once told me that "The Lord is never in a hurry, but He's never late." I had no idea how long He'd keep me on "Hold" but I learned to accept His time schedule even when it was different from mine.

Although I had lived in that apartment for thirteen years and enjoyed it very much, I wasn't sentimental about leaving it. I was too excited about the "Unknown" that was ahead. I only knew that I was to follow Him and He would give me the grace to accept His call. That is what He asks all of us to do, but up until now I hadn't known the meaning of those words. I thought they were for other people at another time. Now, I didn't have to know or understand what was happening. I was free at last to do His work, without any worry about raising a family, earning a living or desiring any of the pleasures that the world had to offer. I was His completely and I rejoiced in the thought — but how little I knew about Jesus at that time.

My first move was a temporary one to Pam Green's small one-bedroom apartment. I knew I needed more solitude than such an arrangement afforded me, so I continued to look for a place of my own. When my two friends, Sisters Verona and Mary Munch heard about my need, they arranged with their sisters at Sacred Heart Academy to permit me the use of a room that could be available to me until August. I accepted their kind invitation, moved into my room and bath in the convent area, and enjoyed the companionship of these good women who lived above the school. I was spiritually enriched, also, by the nearness of the chapel to my room. I couldn't have asked for a quieter or holier place. It was ideal for unraveling my dream and learning to walk with God. During my stay with the sisters, I was still employed by the Board of Education. I had requested retirement in July, 1978.

Before leaving my job, my school clerks gave me a beautiful retirement dinner at which they presented me with a generous cash gift to help with the expenses of starting my Home. Nothing they could have given me would have been more appreciated. I needed funds for the many unexpected expenses involved. It was a beautiful party that I shared with them, many of whom had been my friends for over thirty-three years of my life. I took a little bit of each of them with me when I left the Board and I still cherish their love and friendship. My own family and many of my friends from Our Lady of Mt. Carmel shared the evening with me. There was nothing sad about retiring, for I was filled with enthusiasm for the future. Beginning again was the name of the game I played.

Chapter 4

IRS TAX EXEMPTION

The Shelter of God's Love was incorporated to serve the handicapped community with independent living facilities in a residential environment. Because of our need to be subsidized by financial gifts, we needed a tax exemption for contributors to our Home. Where do I go and how do I apply for it?

This time my daughter-in-law, Mary Koenig, came to my assistance. She directed me to Miriam Sanchez, a contact person in the office of the Lawyers Committee on Civil Rights. One of the functions of this committee is to assist non-profit organizations in obtaining their tax exemption.

Miriam listened to my story, understood my concern and sensed my need for guidance. She told me to send in a written proposal of what I wanted the program to accomplish. She was enthusiastic about my dream and said she was quite sure that the other members of the committee would approve it also. Their approval would guarantee the help I needed. As soon as possible I submitted the material Miriam requested and within a short time she called to tell me the committee had accepted my proposal. She set up an appointment for me to go with her to meet the lawyer who would be handling our case. She told me where his office was located, but I listened rather inattentively as I was going with Miriam and knew she would know where to go. However, things worked out differently. The day of the appointment I drove to Miriam's office to pick her up. Miriam was not there and her office knew nothing about her schedule. For a brief moment, panic seized me. I didn't know who I was to meet or where I was to meet him. My sub-conscious mind took over and I began following some strange leads.

I vaguely remembered Miriam mentioning 111 East Wacker Dr., so I went to a phone directory and going down the list of lawyers, I found a name that sounded familiar — Ned Robertson at that address. I started out for 111 E. Wacker to find him. When I entered the lobby I was aghast to see about six wall-sized directories of the personnel in the building. Looking through the names I could not find Ned Robertson, so I asked the gentleman at the information desk where I might find him. He replied, "What is the name of his law firm?" "I don't know," I answered. "I only know that he's in this building." "Lady, unless you know the name of the law office," he replied, "it will be impossible for you to locate him among all these names." Another "gong" came through from my sub-conscious. "Does this building have thirty floors?" "Yes," said the man. "The law firm of Antonow and Fink occupies the entire thirtieth floor."

All of a sudden I knew where I was going for that was the firm and the floor I had heard Miriam mention. Feeling as though I had made a great discovery, I grinned to myself as I strutted to the elevators, hit the "up" button, then walked into the elevator with great dignity (as if I knew all the time where I was going). I got off at the thirtieth floor, walked to the reception desk and said, "I'm Mrs. Koenig, I have an appointment with Mr. Robertson."

Ned Robertson's generous volunteer service to the Shelter of God's Love began on that day in June, 1978. After much tedious work and reams of correspondence with the IRS in Washington, we received our Foundation Status Classification on May 18, 1979. It was an advance ruling that would end on August 31, 1980 when we would have to send in further confirmation that we had met the requirements of the applicable support test.

When the exemption came through I had difficulty in understanding exactly what was involved. I called Mr. Robertson and asked him to explain what it all meant. He said, "It means you were denied the classification you requested, but received one that is much better. Because of the social security money you will be receiving from the residents you are classified as a publicly supported organization, rather than a privately funded one."

Once more, I just looked up and said, "Thank you, God. You did it again.'' I then asked Him to thank Mr. Robertson for us.

I learned later that Miriam had left hurriedly without word to anyone. She was called home to take her sister to the hospital where she was about to deliver her first baby — Miriam's first niece. All was forgiven — and I thanked Miriam for introducing me to Ned Robertson.

Chapter 5

MY COCOON

After my three months residency in the convent of the Sacred Heart, I had to find other living quarters. More nuns were arriving for the fall school term and they would be needing my rooms. Because I was familiar with the neighborhood and felt very comfortable within walking distance of Loyola's prayer meeting on Thursday night and Wright Hall for my daily mass, I did not want to leave the area, so I began my search for an apartment nearby. I was limited in my choice, for I did not want to take a lease, and apartments without leases were not always the most desirable. I was fortunate when my apartment search began and ended at the Sovereign Hotel two blocks from the convent.

The management called my place an efficiency apartment, but I called it my cocoon. The kitchen sink, stove and refrigerator were all behind a folding screen and all my living, eating and sleeping accommodations were in the one room - truly a room without a view. The only thing I could see from my window was the roof of the swimming pool which obstructed even my view of the alley. It was quite different from my former view of boats in the harbor — but I loved my little hermitage. I had nothing to look at and heard no noises that disturbed me. I enjoyed the quiet that I needed while waiting and praying for the realization of my dream. The greater the distance between me and the sights and sounds of the city, the closer I could be to my God in the solitude of my morning visits. With my mind quiet and my body relaxed I was very much aware of His presence in my solitude.

After my time of prayer and meditation, I'd go to the pool for a swim. I didn't want my inactivity to slow me down. Swimming was the exercise I needed to keep me from pre-senility deterioration. After my swim, shower and breakfast, I'd top off my morning schedule with daily mass. The remainder of my day was spent house hunting and convent chasing for a building in which to open the Shelter of God's Love.

After about six months at the Hotel, I talked to the management about the excessive rent I was paying for such a small living space. He told me that it was because I wouldn't sign a lease. I explained why I needed to be free from a lease when my building became available. He said, "Couldn't you take a six months lease? If you do, I can lower the rent." I said, "I guess I can, because I don't think I'll be moving much before then." I was beginning to realize that God's time table was different from mine. I didn't know at the time that when my lease ended on September 30th, I'd be moving into St. Andrew's Convent on October 1st.

I recalled the words of Joshua 15, "I will not leave you nor forsake you." He was leading me and I must follow in love and trust.

Chapter 6
POSTAL PERMIT

Before we were able to develop a fund raising program, we needed a special postal permit for bulk mailing. In my exploration of a new area, I began asking a lot of questions about procedure in obtaining this special rate. I was directed to an office in the main post office where a gentleman sat, surrounded by the intrigue of a government bureaucracy. Aware of the pseudo dignity of his office, I entered precariously and introduced myself and my reason for the visit. The man wasn't as harsh as I first thought. He sensed my uneasiness and was patient and understanding.

I brought with me all the necessary papers which included my Charter and informative brochures about our program. I was not surprised at his apprehension regarding my credibility. He said, "Why should I give you a permit? You don't have any program in operation." I replied, "I'll never have a program without a postal permit. We need fund raising to start the Home, and we need a postal permit to start fund raising. We cannot afford any other kind of solicitation." THAT look came over his face, the look that said nothing but spoke in a loud silence about tolerance toward a little old lady's eccentric goals. They were all kind to me, so I didn't mind being considered strange. I wanted what I wanted and I knew that with God's help I'd get it.

It was always amusing to me how many intelligent people thought that I was crazy because I was old and attempting to do something new. I recalled my granddaughter's comment the day she told me I was too old to ride a bike. It was fun to know that I didn't fit into that old-age mold reserved for the retired. I was glad there were so many of us who defied senility until we were beyond knowing that we were senile. I was in no hurry for the classification, so I ignored the behavioral pattern that goes along with it.

The post office was not passing out permits indiscriminately but the man was kind enough to consider my request with the written stipulation that the permit would be revoked if the Home was not in operation within the next 18 months. I didn't care what the conditions were. I knew my Heavenly father would meet all my deadlines.

Within the month I received the coveted official permit number allowing us to mail our brochures at a reduced rate after paying an annual fee of $30.00. We were off and running with name, charter and permit.

Chapter 7
CONVENT CHASING

With my paper work completed, I began my search for a building. I felt a convent building would be most adaptable to unrelated adults living together since they were built for such a purpose. I went to the Archdiocese of Chicago to get information regarding school closings. I concluded that if a school was to be closed, the convent might be empty and available. I talked to a gentleman in the real estate department of the Chancery Office, and once again, was greeted with THAT look which I had learned to ignore. I wanted a building and didn't care what anyone thought of me or my dream.

After listening to my story, the man at the Chancery Office said, "I'll keep my eyes and ears open and will let you know as soon as I hear anything." I didn't realize how vague that statement was for it was a long time before I heard anything from him. When I called to remind him of his words, he said, "Every time I see Monsignor Koenig I think of you and your request." My response was, "I hope you see him often then because I am anxious to get started."

Whenever I'd hear about a parish where the school program was to be discontinued, I'd follow through with a visit to the neighborhood. If the convent looked accessible, I'd make an appointment to talk to the pastor. I wasn't always the one rejected. Many of the convents were rejected by me because of size, location, and in some instances by the attitude of the pastors.

I remember one such place in an impoverished suburb. Buildings in the neighborhood were boarded up and the area was desolate with very few people living within the boundaries of the parish. It was a neighborhood I'd be afraid to live in. It was not one in which I would house defenseless handicapped. The pastor, however, gave me the third degree in questioning my ability to support his beautiful building. I told him, "I have very little money, but because it is God's program, I am trusting Him for the necessary funds as they are needed." In his ledger sheet of checks and balances, I didn't balance, nor did he, according to my thinking. I could almost see the reason for such desolation. This man was too practical to depend entirely on Divine Providence. As pastor, he believed the finances of the parish were strictly his responsibility, and I was too great a risk. I knew I would have to be accountable for the home I wanted to establish, but I trusted God to do for me what I was unable to do in the area of financing. Because of my faith in Him I was never disappointed. I knew that someday there would be a Shelter of God's Love. "Your Father knows what you need before you ask him" (Mt. 6:8).

My assuredness didn't make sense, even at times to me, for I had nothing to be confident about, except that deep inner conviction of the need, the dream, and the words from Joshua 1:8. I knew God would find both the building and the finances if I continued to trust Him. I think God drew many people to Himself by vindicating me in many situations that validated my trust in Him.

Chapter 8
A HOUSE ON LONGWOOD DRIVE

A s I sat in my cocoon dreaming of what, someday, would be a residential home for the handicapped, the phone rang. It was my friend, Therese Smith. "Hi, Rosemary. I just found out about a beautiful house for sale on the south side. Are you set on any particular location for your Home?" "Not really," I replied. Therese continued, "There is a lovely big home on Longwood Drive near 103rd Street that has been used as a retirement home. It is being sold for $79,000 and would be ideal for you." "Only $79,000?" I said, as I thought of the distance between that amount and my gross worth which was under $5,000. Therese was ecstatic as she added, "On the north side this place would go for about $200,000." The price was right — my tangible assets were not.

The next day a couple of friends went with me to see the house and we fell in love with it. I was sure we had found the building for our handicapped, so I asked Florence, the realtor about my chances of being considered for it. Florence said, "We have taken a deposit on the house and if the man is able to get a mortgage, the place will be his. I'll call you if the deal falls through." Her words sounded encouraging, but I got the same unspoken message from her as I got from others. "A nice little old lady, but crazy." Ignoring her dubious reaction, I felt that my house hunting was over so I proceeded with the details of my paper work.

My unchartered future was exciting and a real tonic for tired blood. It was cheaper and better than Geritol.

Chapter 9
ONE HOME LOST — ANOTHER HOME FOUND

A lmost a year had passed since my retirement and I still didn't have a building in which to start my program. I called Florence, the realtor who was surprised and disturbed to hear me ask, "What's happening with the house on Longwood Drive?" "I'm sorry, Rosemary. I should have called you. That house was sold over three months ago." "I wish you had called," I replied. "I've been waiting to hear from you and have done nothing about looking for another place."

At their next meeting, I told my Board about my conversation with Florence. I explained to them that I had to get the program started. I couldn't keep talking about something and show no signs of accomplishment. I told them I wanted to rent a three or four bedroom house and get started on something before all our permits, etc. would expire. With their OK, the following day I visited realtors and obtained listings while telling them of my need.

Among the groups with whom I worked, I recruited a powerful prayer team of the best pray-ers in Chicago. They all prayed for the realization of my dream and many were at our first fund raiser. In addition to the financial support I received from them I think their most important contribution was backing me in prayers. I am sure all that happened to make this dream a reality came about because we asked God to show us the way and make us wise enough to trust Him, without reservation. This we did.

During these years I was a member of the Loyola Mundelein prayer group. At every meeting, during the liturgy when extending God's peace to one another, Sr. Beata embraced me in His love after first calling me "Dreamer." I said, "You wait, someday, somewhere the Shelter of God's Love will be opened." She really didn't doubt, she liked to tease me as my wait for a building was now in its second year with time running out on some of my government permits.

The night following our Board meeting, at a Loyola Mundelein prayer meeting, Sr. Beata didn't call me "Dreamer" as she had been doing. Instead she told me about St. Andrew's convent being empty and for rent. She told me that she knew Monsignor John Quinn, the pastor, and thought he would be open to our use of it for the handicapped. I could almost see the light at the end of the tunnel. The following morning when I went to see Monsignor Quinn and found him excited about my dream, I felt as though my search had ended. I was flying high without any stimulant. Monsignor told me the convent needed decorating and quite a bit of work before it would be suitable for our purposes, but that didn't stop me from planning. I assured him that we would take care of all the work necessary.

After our tour of the convent, Monsignor Quinn took me to the rectory saying that he would call the Chancery Office and have them draw up a ten year lease. I sat in his office while he spoke to the gentleman in the real estate office of the Archdiocese. After his conversation, he returned to me and said, "I'll have to call you next week. I understand there are other groups interested in renting the building, and I'll have to discuss the matter with my parish council." My dream suddenly became a nightmare. All hope was gone and for the first time I felt dejected and forgotten by the God whose work I thought I was doing.

When I left the rectory, being the weeping willow that I am, I cried all the way to the Mustard Seed Christian Bookstore, owned and operated by Phil Bujnowski, one of my Board members. As I sobbed out the last of the tears that were in me, I said, "Phil, I had a building and lost it in about ten minutes time." He just said, "Do you want to pray about it?" I said, "Yes" and as we prayed the record on his stereo sang out the words, "See, upon the palms of my hands I have written your name" (Isaiah 49:16). My sadness turned to laughter as I said to Phil, "Do you hear what's on the record?" We both laughed and the tension was over. I was sure that if the Lord wanted me to be at St. Andrew's convent, I'd be there. If He didn't, then I didn't want to be there. After praying with Phil and being consoled by the words of the song, I went home ready to accept whatever was the Lord's Will.

I was so at peace, that I wrote to Monsignor Quinn and told him he didn't have to get in touch with me later in the week. It was quite clear to me that the Archdiocese did not want us to rent the convent. "The Shelter will be opened someday, somewhere," I said, "and when it is, I would appreciate your celebrating the liturgy for the residents because of your enthusiasm for the program." The Archdiocese I am sure, did not object to my helping the handicapped, but they considered me a poor risk, and did not want to have to pick up the pieces of my failure at a time when Catholic Charities could do no more than what they were then doing.

When Monsignor Quinn received my letter he phoned me saying, "Who told you you wouldn't be coming to St Andrew's? The only change is in the duration of the lease, but you are coming to our parish. Because I am retiring in five years and cannot commit my successor to the Shelter, I can only give you a yearly lease."

Once again, "Thank you, God for a pastor with the convictions of Monsignor Quinn and thank you for a convent which will be ideal for your Home for the Handicapped." My good Lord shook me up from time to time, but He never let me down. He reminded me He was the director and still the Man in charge.

Chapter 10
WE HAVE OUR BUILDING

Our lease on St. Andrew's Convent began on October 1, 1979. That was the day after the termination of my lease at the Sovereign Hotel - the six months' lease that I signed in April to obtain a reduction in my rent.

On that day Peg Ahern, Veronica Hill and I moved into the big, big, building that echoed the silence of its emptiness. The building had three floors and approximately forty-two rooms, exclusive of storerooms and bathrooms. We each selected the two rooms we wanted to occupy and began unpacking our belongings. Veronica wanted to be on the first floor, Peg and I went to the second.

It was all soooooo exciting for a while. Then we found out that none of us were the living dolls we thought we were. As we rubbed elbows in the daily confrontation of community living, the Shelter of God's Love was not entirely what the name implied. There was trouble in Paradise.

During the first two months, we had volunteers in our home, painting, plastering and cleaning from morning until night. A ramp was being built and bathrooms were being remodeled to accommodate the needs of the handicapped. The work material (ladders, planks, paint, etc.) was all over the house and the hubbub of the many workers was utter bedlam which made our living together almost impossible. Almost every other week Veronica would send me out to look for an apartment for her, saying, "I'm too old for this sort of living. God doesn't expect me to live like this at my age." As soon as I'd find a place that might be suitable for her needs and finances, she'd change her mind, saying: "I think I'll give it a little more time." Peg, angered one day at something I did or didn't do, ordered me out of the house. I don't know how she would have managed if I had obeyed her command. Community living is never easy but under these conditions it was most difficult. Added to all this confusion I suffered my first attack of angina. It frightened me a little because I was thriving on the excitement and didn't want to be called out of it.

The memories of those two months of living in plaster dust with wooden planks, bathroom tiles and fixtures all over the place makes me grateful for the memory, but I'm not anxious for a repeat performance.

My son Jack did all the remodeling of the bathrooms as well as the building of the ramp. Before I was thinking about such a home, God had sent me my carpenter in the person of my oldest son who was both willing and able to do our remodeling. Our other volunteers came from Our Lady of Mt. Carmel Committee on Community Life and Young Adults Club. Our wash and wear crew were women who came to the house in the evening after working all day. Some were nuns and members of our prayer groups, others were from Mt. Carmel, some were family, all were friends. They worked together washing curtains, windows and woodwork as they put the finishing touches on the freshly painted rooms. In a forty-two room convent this was a big job, but they all enjoyed being part of a dream.

The husband and wife team of Don and Kathy Lux from CCL headed up a work crew of about fifty people in a weekend Work-A-Thon. Don directed the assignment of work and the purchase of material; Kathy was in charge of feeding the workers and keeping them happy while they worked. It was a weekend of frenzied activity that left everyone exhausted but joyful.

Through it all, Peg, Veronica and I were doing our best to understand one another while storming heaven for patience. Tensions were great and our dispositions snapped at the slightest provocation. But the more disturbed we were the harder we had to pray for God's help. We all knew we wanted to be where we were, so we kept trying to understand ourselves and each other a little better. I never wanted out, but I did spend an awful lot of time on my knees. I couldn't walk out on a dream so I embraced it and was able to survive.

During this time of preparation my foot was the recipient of a gallon of paint which fell across my instep. I was taken to Evanston Hospital where I was met by my daughter, Mary Lou, an R.N. employed there. When the people were taking the X-ray, they asked if there was anything else they should check. Mary Lou, without hesitation said, "Yes, maybe you should give her a brain scan while you're at it." They didn't think that was necessary, but they did put my broken foot in a cast.

About a week before our scheduled Open House, Monsignor Quinn stopped over to see how things were going. He looked at the debris in the house, glanced at my foot encased in the cast and in a slightly disturbed, but gentle manner asked, "Do you think it will be ready for the Open House next week?" I assured him it would, as I hobbled along on my broken foot. His response was non-verbal, but I understood his thoughts and fears.

On the Saturday before the festivities, my son, Harry, was busy sanding and waxing the floors, and on Sunday morning workers were still hanging pictures and adding the finishing touches to the beauty of our residence.

At 3:00 p.m. on December 9, 1979 hundreds of our friends and supporters joined us in the celebration which signaled the opening of the Shelter of God's Love. The afternoon began with a Mass of Thanksgiving concelebrated by eight priests in St. Andrew's Chapel. It was followed by a mouth-watering buffet and reception in the Shelter which was hosted by our Intercessory Prayer Group. Our visitors rejoiced with us as they toured our spic and span building and witnessed the power of God's love and His commitment to His program. His beloved disabled had a place to call their own.

Chapter 11

WE BECOME VISIBLE

Once the Shelter of God's Love became acceptable as a new concept of living for the physically handicapped we received much publicity from the news media and television. The first such item was a beautiful article about our Home written by Roy Larson in the Chicago Sun-Times. Roy's report on his visit to the Shelter was a tender and loving story of the beginning and the realization of my dream. At the time of his visit there were only three residents, but Mr. Larson sensed the peace and joy within the home and was aware of God's presence in the Shelter of God's Love. Many of our visitors felt this way, but none expressed it more beautifully than he. He concluded the article with the words, "You can have breakfast at Tiffany's — if you like, but I'd rather have breakfast at the Shelter of God's Love. I like to take my coffee 'with' — with joy, that is.''

Mr. Larson's article prompted the interest of others in the news media and the Shelter began receiving approval and awards from various sources. Although many articles have been written about our program and I have received many awards for my work in the Shelter, I do not cling to such recognition as justly deserved. I know to whom the credit is due, and even though people sometimes misinterpret my attitude, I know what I have done has been too easy to be praiseworthy. I only thank God for the grace which inspired me to open the Shelter of God's Love. A minister once said, "Take all the praise and honor you can get. Then at night when you return to the silence and solitude of your room, give it all back to Him." This is my response to recognition.

My first appearance on TV was as a guest on the "Everyman" show which is a presentation of the Church Federation of Greater Chicago. I was interviewed by its director, Lydia Talbot who believed strongly in what the Home represented. Lydia is a beautiful woman interested and involved in all areas where social justice is an issue. I was very happy and proud to be on such a program. Her questions brought out to the audience the true Spirit of God in my dream.

Shortly after that program, we were invited to be on a television news program. I agreed, with the understanding that I be permitted to speak of God and His action in the lives of the handicapped. I was assured by the moderator that that would be no problem. I learned later that it wasn't any problem for the moderator. However, the editor had sharp shears and cut out everything that, in his opinion, was offensive to the Godless segment of our audience.

The arrival of the television crew and all their paraphernalia created much excitement among our residents. Our house was a beehive of activity for about three hours as they set up their cameras and sound affects. About an hour of that time was spent talking to me and the residents. After they left and our house quieted down once again, we laughed as we recalled some of our responses to their questions. We concluded that we were camera shy and worried about how we would look on television. It was with mixed emotions that we patiently awaited the premier showing of the Shelter of God's Love on the evening news. We had a lot of fun, giggling and laughing in nervous anticipation of our first claim to television fame.

The time allotted us had been five minutes. All of our families and friends had been notified and we knew the whole world would be watching with us. BUT, President Reagan arrived in Chicago at the time of our telecast. Yes, you guessed it. "The Man of the Hour" was Mr. President and the MAN in our lives was deprived of the center stage we wanted to give Him. Our five minutes became three minutes and our message was very dull. No mention of God, nor of His work in the Shelter. We had wanted to use the media to proclaim God's greatness in our lives, but none of our real thoughts or words remained after editing. I'll give one very vivid example of the kind of deletions to which I refer. The moderator, when interviewing one of our youngest residents asked why she was so happy. Marie replied, "Because I have two nice rooms and I love God so much for all He's giving me." What came out of the telecast was, "Because I have two nice rooms."

After the telecast I wrote to the station and told them of my disappointment at their deliberate omission of the spiritual aspects of our Home. I was shocked when in answer to my letter I was told, "We can't offend the civil rights of our audience by highlighting the spiritual side of your program." I replied, "We didn't ask you to highlight, but we are a non-denominational Christian community and should have been referred to as such. There are many things on radio and television that are offensive to my beliefs. Why aren't they cut from the telecasts?" I learned from that, that my convictions were being tested and my right to express them was denied. If they wanted to put my God on a back burner, then I decided to remain there with Him. Fully aware of the repudiation of my rights of expression I have consistently refused to be taped for any television show that is not of a religious origin.

Since this was a new concept of independent living for the physically handicapped, I wanted as much publicity as we could get. However, I'd rather have no publicity than that which denies the importance of God's action in our lives. The Shelter of God's Love gives independence and dignity to handicapped people under the loving protection of our heavenly Father. That was and still is our purpose and goal.

Chapter 12
ALL THE WAY FROM AFRICA

One afternoon, Father Parker, one of our parish priests brought a nun to our home asking if she could stay with us until the next morning when Monsignor Quinn would be returning to the rectory. Sister Carmel was on assignment in the States to raise money for the support of her order's work in the African missions. Father Parker was not familiar with the arrangements Monsignor Quinn had made for her to stay at a nearby retreat center, when Sister had arrived a day earlier than her schedule indicated.

Since we have two rooms with an adjoining bath which I keep for guests, I told Father Parker that Sister could remain with us for the duration of her visit. We needed no money and she would be no burden to us. To me it was an opportunity for the Shelter of God's Love to share in the work of the African missions.

The next day when Monsignor Quinn returned, he called to say he would take Sister to the Cenacle where he had made arrangements for her to stay. I said, "Father, there is no reason why she can't stay at the Shelter. We have the room and the food and we are glad to have her with us. It is all right with her if it meets with your approval." Monsignor Quinn readily agreed if it wouldn't inconvenience us. I assured him that it wouldn't. We were already enjoying her humor and her stories about Africa.

Sister was to visit different churches assigned to her by the Propagation of the Faith. At the masses on Saturday and Sunday she spoke to the people about her religious order's need of financial help from the States. One of the parishes on her schedule was the one in the impoverished suburb of which I spoke earlier in my chapter on convent chasing. I knew that the money received from such a church would be very minimal — and it was. Could it be that God wanted His message of Divine Providence to be taken to the pastor? I asked Sister Carmel to take along some of our newsletters when she went to his parish. I wanted her to give them to the pastor with the word of what God was doing in the Shelter of God's Love. Tell this man who limited God within my inadequacies, that the lady who had no money nor credibility is now living in a convent rented from St. Andrew's Parish. Tell him that our Heavenly Father has given us all that we need as I share my life and His love with eight handicapped people — all of us living in the luxury of Divine Providence.

Sister relayed my message to him. The pastor said he remembered me. He then pointed to his empty convent, saying that it was still empty. Do you believe as I do that God had a hand in this object lesson?

During Sister Carmel's stay in Chicago her weekdays were free — and she used them to good advantage in helping the handicapped. Her special service was sewing and mending. Every hem was turned up and every button sewed on during her three months stay. Because of her simplicity and genial manner, Jeannette Cavender and Ray Nickels, two of our Board members became very fond of our "Blue Nun" — so nicknamed because of her beautiful blue habit. They gave her a tourist's view of the city while making her a real Cub fan. Sister saw her first of many major league ball games while in Chicago. By the time she returned to Africa she was a real "Bleacher Bum" carrying with her a Cub's T-shirt with the name "Blue Nun" imprinted across the front of it.

Our Shelter was blessed by her presence and we were saddened when she left us.

Chapter 13
GIFTS OF DIVINE PROVIDENCE

I cannot devote an entire chapter to each of the many gifts we have received, so I will group many of them together as I tell you of the generosity of Divine Providence. I know all who have helped us have been encouraged to do so because God's love and compassion has touched them and called them to be a part of His Home for the handicapped.

Recognizing the hand of God in the gifts that have been given to us adds to the joy of receiving them. It is thrilling to know that the same God who is the Creator and Controller of all in the heavens above and the earth below is aware and concerned about our little operation.

One of the first gifts received was a beautiful new wheelchair brought to us by Pete Zonzius as a gift from the St. Vincent DePaul Society. At the time I didn't know the price of such an item, nor did I realize how much we needed it. I was constantly being reminded of the way God cared for us. The chair was an important, and as I found out later, very expensive gift. As the years unfolded we became the recipients of many more wheel-chairs - not new, but usable for our monthly prayer meetings. Kevin Shuttleworth, a graduate of St. Andrew's school brought us many wheelchairs he found discarded by a nursing home when it had replaced its old chairs with new ones. It has been said, that one man's garbage is another man's gold. It was not gold we found in the discard; it was God's love for us that kept people aware of our needs.

Roberta Washburn, a member of OLMC Committee on Community Life convinced a friend of hers to give us 36 square yards of beautiful carpet and padding. The gentleman had bought a condo and didn't like the color of the carpet, so his gift made it possible for us to provide our guests with a genuine red carpet welcome to our home. Carpeting also came from many other individuals as well as from St. Andrew's school and rectory. From the school we received enough indoor-outdoor carpeting for 12 resident's rooms. From the rectory we received carpet for our beautiful circular stairway to the third floor. With all this carpeting given to us, it was no surprise to me that the Lord would send someone to lay it.

As I answered the door one day, the caller said, "Aren't you Rosemary Rach from the Academy of Our Lady?" I looked at someone I hadn't seen in over forty years when she introduced herself as a former classmate of mine. I took her through the house and talked to her about the program. At that time we had some carpeting rolled up in the corridor. I spoke of the gift we had received, saying, "Now we have to find someone to put it down for us." Mary replied, "That should be no problem. My husband is in that business. I am sure he will take care of it for you." Her husband was willing also to pick up the donated red carpet from the donor who lived a great distance from us. Once again my unseen Director had spoken. Her visit also renewed my friendship with one whom I had shared my life many years ago as a resident student at the Academy.

One afternoon a gentleman from the Little Brothers brought a handicapped woman to see our house. On that occasion our refrigerator had stopped working and it was beyond repair. The man expressed sympathy, but gave us no solution. The following morning I got a call from the Little Brothers saying, "I understand that you are without a refrigerator." "That's right," I answered. "Ours decided not to work for us any more." He said, "We are picking up a refrigerator at the Hancock Building this morning. If you can use it, we'll bring it directly to you and discard your old one for you." No one had to tell me who had prompted him to offer us the refrigerator. My unseen Director was becoming more visible each day.

On another occasion, John B., one of the officers of the Apostolate of the Handicapped, visited our home and because of his familiarity with the needs of the handicapped, we talked about hand railings for the halls. A few days later, I received a call from John saying, "I have a friend who is a retired carpenter. Could I help you by having him install railings in your corridors? I'll take care of the expenses involved." To myself I said, "Thank you, God." To John, I said, "I'd really appreciate it, John. Just let me know when it will be convenient for him to do the work."

The Shelter of God's Love continues to receive innumerable gifts which are needed in our home. We have received furniture which has filled our house with sofas, a sofa-bed, TVs, desks, beds, kitchen appliances and utensils, dishes, lamps, calculators, typewriters, etc. We have even received a hospital bed equipped with a trapeze and sides which can be used by an individual who is unable to get up from bed without help. We receive clothing of all kinds which we offer to our residents, then to the handicapped friends who attend our monthly prayer meetings. We sell nothing and as fast as we give away what we cannot use, more comes into our house. Clothing that is not taken by our residents or handicapped is then given to a clothing distribution center where others can share God's generosity with us.

Chapter 14

DIVINE PROVIDENCE
Chair Elevator

As our handicapped family grew they needed accessibility to the second floor chapel, community room and bedrooms. The Board was considering an appeal to a private foundation for money for an elevator, but seemed to be dragging their feet in writing the proposal. I told them I thought the Lord wanted us to continue seeking financial help from His people because He wanted more individuals to be a part of the work He was doing in the Shelter of God's Love.

About a week after I had expressed these thoughts to the Board, a friend of mine came to see the house. After her tour of our home, she gave me a check for which I thanked her and set it aside for deposit later. After Joan left, I discovered the check was for $1,000! Not being accustomed to receiving checks in this amount, I immediately called to tell her of my gratitude. Joan said, "I sold my house in Michigan and the Lord told me to bring you that amount for your elevator." She continued, "I tried to talk Him out of giving you the one lump sum, but the Lord was explicit in specifying the amount. So I just said, Yes, Lord, and made the check out for that amount." Knowing that Joan was Charismatic, the message didn't surprise me, for we Charismatics often hear the Lord guiding and directing us. I just repeated my thanks to Joan — and that was the start of our elevator drive.

I called a special Board meeting to tell them what had happened "I don't need any further confirmation," I said. "We will go to our people for the money." Without further delay, Chuck Kramer, one of our very talented Board members, put together a fund raising brochure for our drive.

On October 16th we received the first returns from the brochure. Each week thereafter, I totaled the receipts and sent the monies on to the treasurer for deposit. On December 12th I totaled the 29 checks ranging from $1.00 to $100.00 that I had received from the first of the month. On that day, when the cash received was added to the amount previously forwarded to our treasurer, we had collected $8,077.00 — what I thought was the exact cost of the elevator. I was not yet a "died in the wool" believer so I had to check my files for a copy of our invoice. I had to see — before I believed — that the funds collected as of December 12th (less than two months after our drive began) were the exact amount of the bill for the elevator!

Our Car

God's action in the Shelter of God's Love was gentle and without fanfare. His presence is the quiet, but firm foundation of our Home.

One morning while lingering over my second cup of coffee, the phone rang and as I answered it with my usual, "Good morning, Shelter of God's Love. May I help you?" I heard a very weak voice respond. "Good morning, Rosemary. I don't think you can help me, but I hope I can help you." Carrie Weissgerber was the caller and she wanted to talk to me about donating her car to the Shelter. Her birthday was in September and she had received notice regarding the renewal of her driver's license. Carrie said, "I'll be 93 years old next month and Our Blessed Mother told me to give my car to the Shelter, because I'm too old to drive." I said to myself, "Thank you, Jesus, for bringing your mother into this program. We need all the help we can get." Trying to keep my voice calm, as though the gift of a car was a common occurrence, I replied, "I'll be happy to talk to you Carrie, and I appreciate your concern for us." Later in the week we set up an appointment when the two of us could meet with our Shelter attorney, Bill Kelly, to confirm the legality of the transfer of title. As a result of that meeting and for the dollar transfer of title fee we were the recipients of a beautiful 1977 4-door Dodge Aspen with air conditioning and snow tires. The car had only been driven 5500 miles.

Carrie, a member of St. Andrew's parish was, told of our need by another parishioner, Evelyn Peterson. Being members of the dynamic parish whose pastor first accepted us, I was not surprised at the compassion shown us by these two women. I was happy, though, to know that Divine Providence anticipated our need even before it was evident to us. I had been driving my 1971 car with 85,000 miles on it and I assumed that God would keep it running until we acquired a much needed van. I didn't expect Him to replace it until that time.

In the summer of 1977 after attending the American Federation of Teachers' convention in Boston, Jeanie Condrella and I rented a Dodge Aspen for a drive through the New England states. I said at that time that my next car was going to be a Dodge Aspen because I liked the way it handled. Little did I realize that Carrie was already purchasing my Aspen for a gift to the Shelter in 1982.

Before the new license was on the car, the Southwest Archdiocesan Singles presented us with another gift of more than $400.00 which paid for our license, vehicle sticker and insurance.

I always got the message that God wanted all of His children to be involved in His program. He ignored the generation gap which had been made so wide and divisive by people's attitudes. Our residents' ages now range from 21 to 80 and our benefactors range from the age of reason to 96. How wonderful is our God who unites us all in His love!

Our Piano

Sometimes I think that the Holy Spirit, rather than Alexander Graham Bell invented the telephone. I'm sure He had something to do with it because almost all our gifts have come to us via Ma Bell. I'm sure Divine Providence has a large staff in the distribution department of heavenly assets, but I don't think delivery would be as efficient without the services of the telephone.

One day a friend of ours while visiting at the Shelter wistfully said, "I wish someone would give you a piano. It would be so nice for everyone, especially when Veronica is able to play so beautifully." With my one-track mind, I answered, "When the Lord has one ready for us, we'll hear about it." Even my friends were beginning to give me THAT look which I was still ignoring.

Later on that same day, Divine Providence in the person of Frances Dirksen, using Ma Bell's instrument of communication, called to inquire if we could use her spinet piano. She was moving to a retirement village and wanted to give us her piano. "It was a wedding gift from my husband," Frances said, "and I'd like to know that it will provide as much pleasure to your residents as it has provided me throughout the years."

I replied, "Frances, you won't believe what I'm going to tell you, but for the record I must repeat a conversation I had this morning with a friend who visited us at the Shelter." My friend, Marie, said she wished we'd get a piano for the residents to enjoy and for Veronica to play. I told her, "When the Lord has one ready, we'll hear about it." That was less than five hours ago, and now your call." No wonder I trust my heavenly Father so completely. He makes it hard for me to do otherwise. I went on to say, "We'll be thrilled to have the piano, Frances, and we appreciate your thinking of us. I'll get someone to pick it up. Could I call you back when I get more information about the pick-up? I'm still stunned by your offer coming so soon after Marie's visit."

My next call was to John McCarthy of Dunn Brothers Storage &Warehouse where I had stored my furniture after moving out of my apartment. In my conversation with Mr. McCarthy, I asked if he would be able to pick up the piano for us. He said he thought he could but he'd have to look over his schedule. He told me Dick Dunn would call me back in the morning. The next day, Mr. Dunn called to inquire about the location of the piano and the phone number of the donor so he could make arrangements for the pick-up. Once again, I was aghast at his generous and prompt response. I said, "I can't tell you how much I appreciate your doing this for us." Mr. Dunn's reply was, "I'm grateful that you asked us to do it." Doesn't that sound "out of this world" for a human response?

Divine Providence is the action — the Holy Spirit is the inspiration. What a great team and how wonderful are the results of such heavenly teamwork!

A few days later the piano arrived and the rafters rang with songs of praise and thanksgiving. Many events have been made joyous because of Frances' gift. Again, thank you God and thank you, Frances, for responding to His voice when He told you of our need.

Saints and Sinners

One Sunday morning I opened the front door to two gentlemen who were complete strangers to me. They had heard about our house and said they belonged to the Saints and Sinners Club and were looking at programs they could offer help to at Christmas time.

I greeted the young men and after talking to them about the purpose and the operation of the home, I took them through the building. I introduced them to the residents - some of whom thought I was very foolish to fall for their story. Our visitors could be plotting to hurt us, they could be going through the home to get the layout, etc., etc. Fear is deadly and inspires some terrible thoughts. Because of their disability the handicapped live in apprehension, and cannot risk being too trusting.

I understood their fears but was annoyed at their lack of trust in my judgement. I believe in being prudent and protective of those under my care, but I'd rather trust God for the ultimate protection under all circumstances. All I saw in these two young people was their concern for the disabled. The name of their group was one of the causes for my residents' concern — Saints and Sinners — which were they?

No harm came to us as they toured our home. They were the epitome of kindness and the idealism of youth. Labels mean nothing to me. I've known many who profess to be saints but are greater sinners than others known by that name. I saw the name of their club as an interesting and credible one. Aren't we all saints and sinners at different times?

About a month after their visit, I received a call from one of the men saying they had approved the Shelter of God's Love as the recipient of a $1,500.00 gift to be used as we saw fit. I gratefully accepted their decision and agreed to be at their Christmas dinner to accept the check.

It gave me great pleasure to tell my residents about our windfall. My family learned an invaluable lesson of accepting people for what they are, rather than for what they might be.

When I attended their Christmas dinner I met many beautiful young people, all of whom I would call saints (the sinners must have remained at home). Their gift to us was great, but its value was magnified by our need. The gift enriched both the giver and receiver, for I believe those who share their gifts with others are truly blessed by our Giver of all gifts, our dear Lord.

We Drive in Style

With the steady growth of the family, our transportation problems had grown also. We were considering the purchase of a large van with a hydraulic lift needed to accommodate residents in wheel-chairs.

Rick Wellbank, one of our residents, heard about a used van that was for sale. Information about it had been posted on the bulletin board at Maine Township High School where Rick was once a student. He learned of it from some friends at the school. Helen

McSloy and I went to look at the vehicle with a very negative attitude about its usefulness.

The owners lived in Park Ridge and the van had been used for transporting their handicapped son who was a victim of muscular dystrophy. The boy had recently died and the van was a sad reminder of their son, so the family wanted to dispose of it as soon as possible. When we saw the vehicle we were excited about it and were ashamed of ourselves for having been so negative about God's direction in our lives. We should have known that He wouldn't give us a false hope. The van was ideal for our family and the price was right for such a beautiful car. Even though we knew we had to get approval from the Board for its purchase, we knew it would be ours. Our Board would have to come up with the ways and means by which we could afford to purchase it. We asked the owner to hold it for the Shelter. "It's exactly what we want," Helen said. He replied: "We will be glad to know that the residents in a home such as yours will be able to enjoy it. We will keep it for you."

A Board meeting was called and it was agreed that we should buy the van. We would raise the money the same way we had in the past, by a special fund raising appeal. Chuck Kramer, our newsletter editor, gathered together all the information needed and put together a very attractive brochure.

Once again we walked in faith and purchased the van with monies from a bank loan. Our trust in Divine Providence has always been vindicated, so within three months we had received all the money needed to pay off the loan. The van was a real buy for only $7,500.00. It had only 29,000 miles on it and was in beautiful condition inside and out. Our name and logo have been placed on both sides of the vehicle, so we do a little advertising for our dear Provider as we enjoy our tours through His city and suburbs in the majestic style befitting children of a king.

A New Freezer

Because the appliances in the convent were old, we found it necessary to replace, rather than repair them as they wore out. According to "Murphy's Law", it was in the middle of the summer when one of our freezers decided it was too tired to continue taking care of our food. It didn't take me long to learn how important it was for me to replace it.

The Board spoke of buying a new freezer, but considered it too expensive for our finances at that time. Jerry Reedy, our Board chairperson suggested that we place an ad in the Sunday bulletin of Our Lady of Mt. Carmel. We would ask the parishioners if any of them had a used freezer that we could buy. The ad read: Wanted to buy - a used freezer for the Shelter of God's Love — A Home for the Physically Handicapped. Please call Rosemary at — - —.

On Monday following publication of our ad I received a call from a man unknown to any of us. He told me to buy a new freezer and have the salesperson call him for confirmation of the purchase and authorization to charge it to his Visa account. After I picked myself up off the floor, I thanked him and said I would shop for one the next day.

The following day, after looking at freezers and finding them quite expensive, I called David and asked him what my limits were. He said, "Your limits are whatever you want them to be." I said, "I'd rather be boxed into some kind of figure." "Any amount between five hundred and a thousand will be OK with me," he replied. Once again I thanked him and asked God to bless him for his generosity.

Within the week I purchased a beautiful 21 cubic foot freezer and gave the clerk David's phone number for confirmation and approval for it to be charged to his Visa account.

A few days later our new freezer was delivered. I have yet to meet our beautiful donor, but I assure you that God knows who he is and in His own way has thanked him again and again for his kindness to us. God is never outdone in generosity.

Evelyn's Window Bars

Even though the convent had been built many years ago at a time when crime and home invasion was not the terror it is today, bars were on all the bedroom windows which were on the alley side of the building. Evelyn Valin's room did not have such protection on her windows as her room had been used as an office, rather than a bedroom. We had no problem with this until one night someone tried to get in the building through her window. A burglar lock kept out the invader, but the incident frightened Evelyn so much that I asked if she wanted to have bars put on her window. Her answer was, "Yes, if they aren't too expensive." I replied, "Your peace of mind and your safety are the first consideration, not the cost involved." At the same time I had all our locks changed as the invader had tried to gain entry through the back door also.

I immediately solicited prices from different shops in the area that installed window bars. Upon making a choice of the place where I would place the order, I arranged to have the work done by the end of the week. The total cost of the bars and the lock changes came to $289.00.

Within that same week, I received a check for $300.00 from a donor who wanted to recognize three of her handicapped friends who were affiliated with the Shelter. One of these was Evelyn Valin, the resident in whose room the bars were installed. The others were Ruth Crigley and Carter Burton, two of our involved Board members.

You might wonder why she sent $300.00. I wasn't surprised. I just said, "Thank you, God and thank you, Anne." I recognized the teamwork of Divine Providence.

A Catalytic Converter Converts Me

One day while on an errand for the Shelter, I found myself driving behind a very noisy van. I thought to myself, I'd better get away from this heap of junk before it falls apart in front of me. As I pulled away from it, the noise seemed to follow me. After a few blocks and a lot of distance between me and the van, I had to conclude that my dear little Aspen was the one breaking the sound barrier. Believing the noise was caused by a faulty muffler, I drove directly to my favorite service station where I was told, "It's not the muffler or anything we can fix. The catalytic converter is your problem and you'll have to take it to your Dodge dealer for repairs." Not being a liberated woman the only parts of a car I was familiar with were the gear shift, brakes, gas pedal and windshield wiper blades, so I was a little concerned about the costs involved. At that time the Shelter of God's Love was having no great problem with surplus funds - there weren't any.

Reluctantly I took my dear car to the Dodge dealer where they told me that the converter would have to be ordered, but the car could still be driven - noisily, yes, but safely. So I drove my Aspen out of the garage with my driver's license close at hand and my work order for the repairs in the glove compartment - just in case the officers of the law thought I was disturbing the peace and quiet of their noisy city.

The officers, however, respecting my senility ignored me and my noise-maker. They probably thought I was too deaf and too old to realize how obnoxious I was. It amused me though when I drove up to a stop light and saw the expressions on the faces of the by-standers. To them, I was a senior hot-rodder — far removed from their image of a woman of my vintage.

While waiting for the part to be delivered I continued to drive the car and even became used to the noise of it. But one day after leaving the expressway and while driving down Irving Park Road, the noise magnified by a thousand decibels, when part of the muffler fell off the car and was scraping along the cement. I thanked God that it didn't happen while I was on the expressway. At this time I was within a mile of the place where my car was to be fixed. My embarrassment prompted me to bury my head in my lap as I drove down the busy street but I found out that wasn't a good position for the head of a driver, so I sat up straight and prayed my way to the Dodge garage.

When I finally reached my destination (the ride was an agonizing one with all the additional clamor from the fallen muffler), I inquired if the converter was in. When they said it was, I asked if they could repair or replace the muffler at the same time. When they replied in the affirmative, I left my car with them and went home on the bus.

While at home that same afternoon Jerry Reedy brought me a check for $500.00 - a gift from the Committee on Community Life who were disbanding their organization and dispersing their assets among other non-profit organizations.

Later in the day when I picked up my car I was given a bill for $242.50. This time Divine Providence overpaid the repair bill and we had money left over to deposit to our account.

It might seem strange to you, but it wasn't to me. I just said, "Thank you, God and thank you Committee on Community Life."

A New Refrigerator

I think the most temperamental appliance in a home is the refrigerator that goes on the blink when the outside temperature soars to the nineties and replacement cannot be postponed until finances are available. I seemed to be having so much fun trusting God for all these things that I was constantly testing Him with new challenges. I wanted to make sure He was still listening to us and providing for our needs. After all He had been taking care of the Shelter family for over six years and might have thought we'd like to try it on our own for a change. NOT ME! I had lived a lifetime of figuring out my income and expenses and let me tell you I like my new accounting system much better. It is much easier on me to know that He knows what we need and sees that we get the money to purchase it.

This attitude is now second nature to me so when our refrigerator passed beyond the "point of no repair" I shopped for a new one. The one I chose cost $528.00.Between the time of purchase and the date of delivery the Shelter received a check for $500.00 which was bequeathed to our Home by a deceased friend of Helen McSloy.

You might think I am embellishing the story with these gifts of Divine Providence. I assure you that every gift can be documented if you care to look at our records. In HIS name we are "Show-offs".

Chapter 15
SHELTER ACTIVITIES

Our charter reads: "The Shelter of God's Love is a family home where physically handicapped work and pray together." It is all that, but much more. It has become a center for many different activities. The first and most important is the Charismatic prayer meeting for what is now known as the Shelter of God's Love Intercessory Prayer Group of which I spoke in a previous chapter. My handicapped friends prayed us into our building and now share our home with us on the third Saturday of each month. It is a time of praise and thanksgiving to our God, followed by a celebration of the Eucharist and an afternoon of fellowship for approximately 45 disabled people who have, throughout the years, become very good friends. Volunteer drivers make the day possible as we answer God's call to help one another. We are enriched by our encounter — first with God, then with our friends.

Prayer meetings are held in our beautiful chapel and I sense the joy of the Lord each time we gather there. Convents have always been a place set aside as an enclosure for God's children who loudly proclaimed His presence in their lives. St. Andrew's convent is now the enclosure for the residents of the Shelter of God's Love who witness to the great love of God that envelops and sustains them in their lay apostolate.

On the second Wednesday of each month, Monsignor Thomas Obrycki, a paraplegic priest comes to our home to celebrate the liturgy for the residents. We are joined on this occasion by several of our friends who are prayer partners with us in asking God's blessing on us, our families, benefactors and parishioners of St. Andrew's parish. Monsignor Obrycki's presence in the Shelter and his ability to perform his priestly functions in spite of his disability is an inspiration to all. His life is truly a reflection of the power of God's love.

On the third Tuesday of each month, Father Charles Rubey from Catholic Charities celebrates the liturgy for our family. At Catholic Charities, Father Rubey works with the families of suicide victims. He has an innate compassion for suffering people so his interest in the handicapped is understandable. When I was in high school, my best friend was Stella O'Kelly who is Father Rubey's mother. I didn't think at the time that we would remain friends for over sixty years and that her son would be so much a part of a dream I hadn't even begun to dream.

On the day Father Rubey comes to the Shelter, we are hosts to about twenty of our friends and benefactors who share our dinner with us prior to the celebration of the liturgy. It is a time of great fellowship and many blessings. There is a wonderful solemnity and joy among friends when they gather in God's name to praise and thank Him for His gifts of life and love. Another Shelter event is our annual Christmas party for the children in the primary grades at St. Andrew's school. I believe it is important that children learn early in life that a handicapped individual should not be made a victim of stares and pity. By our attitudes we sometimes dwell more on our differences than on our similarities, and those differences divide us. I want the little ones to know the handicapped as persons very much like themselves. They need our physical assistance and we need their prayers - so we need each other.

During their visit I talk to the children about their disabled neighbors in the Shelter and I ask them to understand and be friendly to them. On one occasion I asked the children if they knew what is meant by a "handicapped persons." The answers were varied, but the one that silenced me was, "A handicapped person is one that God made a mistake on." I was a bit taken back by this response, so I just replied, "God doesn't make mistakes." I explained that through His disabled ones He gives us the opportunity to become closer to Him. They didn't quite understand that so I quoted from the Bible about the man born blind. When the disciples asked our Lord, "Rabbi, was it his sin or that of his parents that caused him to be born blind?" "Neither," answered Jesus: ". . . . .It was to let God's works show forth in him." (John 9:3) I then asked them, "Doesn't that make them very special people?" So whenever you push a wheelchair, help a blind person cross the street, or even when you just smile and say 'Hi' to a crippled person, then you, too, are one of God's workers - and that's what we should all want to be.

After our little talk in the community room and a tour of our home, we return to the dining room where each child is given a candy bar and a dixie cup from our residents and then receives a gift from Santa Claus, Kevin Shuttleworth, who many years ago was one of St. Andrew's school children.

I pray that our young students will grow up to be real witnesses of God's love in their lives - because they met His handicapped in the Shelter of God's Love.

Chapter 16

OUR INTERCESSORY PRAYERS

For The Living — The Infant's Crib

Every day the residents pray together in thanksgiving for our home and our benefactors, and we lift up to God the needs of our families and friends. From the time the Shelter opened its doors this has been a pattern of our Christian community. But one day a friend told me about the manner in which she prays, especially when troubled. Marion said, "I always keep in mind the image of the Infant in His crib. When something is bothering me or when I need guidance in raising my boys, I place that need in my faith crib and trust the Infant to help me through my difficulties. In this way, I don't carry the burden with me throughout the day. I release it to the Lord knowing that He will handle it."

Marion's imagery was so beautiful, and since I am not one to let any such idea die on the drawing board, we now have placed the Infant in a real (doll) crib under the picture of the Madonna and Child in our dining room.

After our daily prayers for our benefactors and for the needs presented to us by our friends, we tuck the petitions in our crib where God's greatest manifestation of His love is evident in the birth of Jesus. We ask God to accept these petitions on behalf of all who have come to us for prayers and for all who are a part of the Shelter.

It is symbolic that in the Shelter of God's Love we have found the tenderness of the Infant, the suffering of our crucified Christ and the peace, joy and hope which is ours in the resurrection of Jesus, our Savior.

For The Deceased — Memorial Plaques

As a family we are very much aware of the needs and hurts of all those who are a part of us. In our Christian community we give and receive much moral as well as physical support from one another. We know, however, that many of our friends are struggling through their suffering with little comfort and spiritual support from their friends.

In our dining room we have three memorial plaques on which are placed the names of the deceased friends and family members of our benefactors. Daily we ask God to take them to His heaven and comfort the loved ones they have left behind. We intercede for our sorrowing friends and ask God to hasten the day when they can accept, without pain, the loneliness of separation from one they loved.

Chapter 17
OUR SHELTER FAMILY
Veronica Hill

Veronica Hill, one of the first residents of the Shelter is now 80 years old and suffering from a malignancy. After hospitalization for radiation treatment, she was transferred three months ago to a nursing home for care that we are unable to provide.

Veronica was a widow who had lived alone for many years. For more than 30 years she was an alcoholic and had known all the despair and isolation of the disease. As a recovered alcoholic, Veronica's charm, love of God and compassion attracts all people, particularly those rejected by society.

When Veronica surrendered her independence and decided to live within the guidelines of the Shelter environment, she found her niche in her sensitivity to the needs of those with whom she lived. As a talented pianist she brought priceless entertainment to us all. Her great sense of humor makes her a fun person to be around. Veronica's sense of humor can be described by relating the story of our spaghetti dinner.

One evening we had company call on us unexpectedly at dinner time, when I found myself a little short of food. Word went out for the family to hold back. While straining the cooked spaghetti (which was in short supply) some spilled into the sink. I washed it and placed it back in the strainer with Veronica watching me. "I'm not eating any of that," she declared. "It won't hurt you," I said. "It's all washed again." "I don't care," said Veronica. "Someone else can have my portion." When dinner was served, I noticed Veronica eating the spaghetti. After the guests left, I reminded her of what she had said. Her response was, "I got to thinking that if all of you died from food poisoning and I was the only survivor, I'd be the one charged with your deaths, so I thought it would be better for me to die with you."

A nursing home to many is that awful place where people are sent to die. Not so with Veronica. Her charm and laughter has brought new life to many of the patients. In fact she is such a good actress that many of the patients in the home tell her she is too healthy to be there. They know differently after she humorously gives them a run down of her ailments. Veronica knows what her physical condition is — but like the handicapped with whom she had lived, she ignores the negatives in her life and with the fire of God's love inspiring her, she serves Him in her disability.

Veronica's rooms are being kept for her return. We are a people of hope.

Peg Ahern

Peg Ahern was the other individual who opened the Shelter with Veronica and me. Peg had lived with her sister for over 28 years and was anxious to try it on her own at the ripe young age of 64. Her golden years were not to be spent in the luxury of a retirement village but in living independently in the Shelter of God's Love with other handicapped residents. At a time when most people end their working careers, Peg was beginning hers as she stepped boldly into a life of challenges.

Peg is a victim of cerebral palsy. She had lived with her parents until their passing, then moved in with her sister, brother-in-law, and their three daughters. Peg is another individual who understands the hurts and disappointments of others because of the difficulties in her own adjustment to life as a disabled person. Her life was not as colorful and exciting as was Veronica's but it was a life of daily walking with God, accepting her disability and enjoying life to the fullest within the limits of her handicap.

During those first hectic months in the Shelter, Peg never wanted out, but I know there were times when she must have wondered about her decision. Because she had already overcome many trials in her life, she was able to weather the storms of inconvenience, and surmount the obstacles she met as a founding resident of the

Shelter.

Peg is now 70 and apart from "yours truly" is the senior member of our family. Peg likes the title, but would prefer to have Veronica back with us brightening up our house with her great sense of humor and salty wisdom. One characteristic of all the residents is their great desire to serve God and to love Him in the joy of their newly found freedom and independence. Peg is a model of patience and an inspiration to all who are a part of the Shelter family. She gives encouragement and appreciation to all who cross her path, while the loving support she receives from the other residents enhances her own life in the Shelter of God's Love.

Marie Ward

Marie Ward, a victim of cerebral palsy came to the Shelter in 1980. Marie is a loving, trusting, saintly young lady for whom the phrase, "Black is Beautiful" must have been coined. No one coming into our home and meeting Marie is left untouched by that encounter.

Until Marie was eleven years old she had lived with her grandmother. At that time her grandmother died and Marie moved into the home of her aunt, Imogene Warren. At 21 years of age she came to the Shelter of God's Love.

When her father died in 1981, our Board attorney, Bill Kelly, told me she should receive a pension from the Railroad Retirement Board since her father had been a railroad employee for over 30 years. As a result of Bill's investigation, Marie now receives a pension which provides her with a few luxuries in her life. She is living independently in her two rooms with her own private phone, many Michael Jackson albums, a few vacation trips with her Aunt Imogene and spending money for the little entertainment that she enjoys.

I recall the time, shortly after Marie came to us, when Veronica left the breakfast table to get her lower dentures. Marie asked where she was going. I replied, "To get her teeth." Marie looked aghast, while saying, "Get her teeth? I never take mine out of my mouth." The generation gap was closed with that statement and to this day we just laugh at one another's strengths and weaknesses in our age differences.

This young lady who had been cared for all her life as a dependent handicapped child is now a mature, beautiful young woman living her own life helping others and being helped by them. Marie is a great Bible scholar and quotes quite freely from it. She lives one day at a time — loving God, loving others, and living physically and spiritually in the Shelter of God's Love.

Rick Wellbank

Rick Wellbank, a truly courageous young man came to the Shelter in 1981. When I first met him I wondered about his ability to live independently because of the severity of his handicap. I learned later that I had no reason for my apprehension because what Rick lacks in physical ability he more than makes up for in spiritual fortitude, sheer determination and a keen sense of humor.

Rick, like Marie, is a Bible scholar. It is inspiring to live with people who find their answers to problems in the reading of scripture. When I hear Rick praying aloud and talking to God in the silence of his room I am reminded always of God's presence in His handicapped. When I hear him, I utter a prayer of gratitude for God's home for His handicapped where His hurt children can share their love of Him with their love for one another.

Rick is now 26 and during his four years in our home the lives of many have been blessed by his smile and his happy, healthy acceptance of his disability. In my work with the disabled I have been privileged to see the hand of God working in and through them. First God touches them with His love, then as they thirst for more, He saturates them with His presence and sends them out to take His love to others.

I have in my Bible a prayer card on which I have written my petitions for the needs of my Shelter family. The petitions were written in 1981 and all but one have been granted - the one I'm waiting on is Rick's healing, and I boldly proclaim that my prayer will be answered, according to God's Holy Will in a way that will enable Rick to function with less difficulty. My Shelter family and friends are adding their prayers to mine as we ask God to bless our young man with a healing.

Evelyn Valin

Evelyn Valin is the widowed mother of six children. She has been handicapped from multiple sclerosis since 1973 and came to the Shelter of God's Love in 1982. Evelyn learned of our home through the Apostolate of the Handicapped. It has been argued that the hardship of being crippled from birth is much easier to accept than to have lived as an able-bodied person most of your life and then through an accident or illness become disabled. I have worked with the handicapped for many years, and have learned from them that a disability of any kind is a heavy cross to carry and the weight of it can only be lightened by help from above. God's love is what insulates the handicapped from much of the hurt and rejection that is a part of their lives.

Evelyn has a wonderful family and counts her blessings for the life that was hers before her illness. She is now Rick's surrogate mother and has found in the Shelter, her seventh child. She is Rick's personal (non-salaried) attendant and we all have many laughs over the way she babies this grown man. We tease her about her ''smother love'' but she just laughs and continues to care for him. Rick is her apostolate in the Shelter, but she has a larger ministry with the handicapped as a member of CUSA (Catholic Union of the Sick of America). Her involvement in this organization consists in corresponding with other ''Shut-ins'' who are members of the same group. This keeps her at the typewriter a good part of each day, but it is a beautiful work done from her wheelchair as she reaches out across the country to others who are also wheelchair bound.

Evelyn's adjustment to taking orders after a lifetime of giving them is a beautiful witness of submission to God's will in her life. In community living, dying to self is one of the most difficult lessons to be learned, but once it is learned, a most beautiful life unfolds.

Marge Motyka

Marge Motyka, a victim of cerebral palsy, came to the Shelter in 1983 when she was 23 years of age. Her physical handicap was the lesser of her problems, even though she was ambulatory only with the aid of crutches. Marge's life had not been a happy one. Because of her parents' inability to care for her she was placed in a foster home when she was very young. Nothing but good, however, came from this placement as her foster family is still very close to Marge. They were instrumental in her coming to the Shelter of God's Love.

Many of us take for granted the blessings of a supportive and loving family and are unaware of the pain of rejection felt by those who are not so fortunate. Marge had a great deal of hurt inside of her which made her fearful of the unknown atmosphere of our home. She wanted to live independently, but she wasn't going to blindly accept house rules that might curtail her independence.

Marge's first weeks were difficult ones. She had such a hunger to love and be loved, but with it she had a deep-seated fear of being hurt if she allowed anyone to touch her life in a caring way. I loved her with the love a mother has for a child. She was so vulnerable, but boldly asserted her right to be an independent 23 year old. It was difficult to convince Marge that my love for her was unconditional. She bristled from any show of affection. I wanted to put my arms around her and heal her hurts, but at the same time I had to respect her determination to be self-reliant.

After a few encounters through an exchange of words, we began to understand each other and Marge settled down to giving us a chance. I'm sure if she had any other place to go she would have left the Shelter, but she was restricted to accepting our hospitality until something better came along.

Eventually something better did come along - but still in the Shelter. Marge began to feel comfortable in her two rooms. She accepted us and became a participating member of our family. It is now two years since Marge came to the Shelter for her own convenience and found that she was making it a nicer place for us, too, as she became an outgoing little lady who is loving and loved by us all. Both of her parents are deceased, but in the Shelter of God's Love she has found others who love her as if she were their own daughter.

God is good. He stayed close during the time we worked through our problems and now we have no problem. Marge Motyka is a happy contributing member of God's Home for His handicapped.

Annette Lencki

A nnette Lencki, handicapped from the birth defect of spina bi-fida, came to the Shelter in 1983. Before that time she had lived in her own apartment after leaving the State Hospital School in 1980. Her salary as an employee of the Spina Bifida Association is minimal, but Annette gets more out of her employment than salary. Her work is a healthy outlet for her gregarious nature. Her ability to communicate and establish rapport with her co-workers makes life enjoyable for her.

Like all other new residents Annette found the adjustment to community living difficult. The name of our home sounds restful and peaceful, but many demands are placed on new residents, sharing their lives with a family of unrelated handicapped adults. Young people don't like rules and until they learn that guidelines are non-restrictive and necessary, they object to obeying them.

Annette was 26 when she came to us. Most of her life was lived at the hospital school. After leaving the school she found her freedom from the jurisdiction of school authority exciting until the novelty wore off and the reality of responsibility sank in. Her parents had neglected to give her the support she needed to adjust to the maturity of adulthood, so she struggled alone toward goals that were unrealistic.

Annette brought all her frustrations and brusqueness to the Shelter of God's Love. She did not understand that she had to relate to the other residents and the rules. It didn't take her long to learn otherwise. She is a very bright and loving individual and when she discarded her cloak of brashness, we could not resist her simple offer of love. Her projected image was that of a worldly-wise, stubborn, handicapped child in an adult body. However, the image was a counterfeit.

After knowing her as a family member of the Shelter for over a year, I cannot say anything but, "Thank you, Annette, for becoming the young lady that you are today." Her hurts from her disability and the rejection by her parents were debilitating, but in the Shelter of God's Love, Annette has been healed from the pain of both. She now basks in the aura of God's love, drawing many to Him through her beautiful smile and sacrificial, but happy life.

Heather Knowles

Heather Knowles, 21 years of age, is the newest and youngest member of the Shelter family. She comes to the Shelter of God's Love from the Illinois Children's Hospital School. Heather is an individual who carries with her many scars of rejection. We have not been able to erase this bitterness from her, but with God's help and the help of the residents, I know that she soon will release her resentments just as the others have.

Heather suffers from the handicap of spina bifida. Her emotional scars are much deeper than the physical handicap that is obvious. The more the handicapped are isolated from the "norm" of society the more their hearts cry out for recognition. The lives of individuals are sometimes shattered by the lack of a loving family structure, but the disabled are totally crushed by the same circumstances. Heather has lost both her mother and her ten-year old brother in violent deaths. While she craves love, she is afraid to accept it.

The Shelter of God's Love was established for just such a person and it is a fun place to be when the presence of God is so visible in the lives of His hurt children. In our home He calls us all to find comfort and strength in His loving arms.

Heather has never lived on her own, so she is intoxicated with her freedom. I am trying to help her to accept the responsibility that accompanies freedom. She is a beautiful young lady covering up her fears and hurts under a pseudo bravado.

I look at Heather and the motto comes to mind, "Human Being, Handle with Care." Yes, Heather does need special handling, but with the track record God has in our home, I know He has placed her there for His own good purposes. I ask for His guidance so that we can help her.

Chapter 18

TILES IN OUR MOSAIC

I conclude my story about the Shelter of God's Love, I must step aside long enough to say "Thank you" to the many people who are the tiles of our mosaic - our Home for the Handicapped. I began the story of my life needing people - I end the story in the same way. I pray that I will always need them, for in God's people I have found my God.

If it were not for Monsignor John S. Quinn, pastor of St. Andrew's parish we would have no story to tell. While others thought I was a senile, mental midget, this man of God must have seen the hand of the Lord in the work I felt called to do. Monsignor Quinn walked in faith with me and opened the doors to our Home by allowing us to rent the unused convent in his parish.

The building is ideal for our purposes, the parishioners receptive and supportive of our Home and the priests happy and cooperative in our needs. While being aware of the work God was doing through me, I was not surprised that He had called Monsignor Quinn into the program. Father is a very influential man - the kind referred to as a "Prophet of Power" in the Old Testament. God's work was successfully carried out by these holy men even when survival was at stake. I admire and thank God for His modern day "Prophet of Power" in the Shelter of God's Love - Monsignor John S. Quinn.

Because we have no government or church support, I am thankful for those contributors who are the corner stone on which our program is built. Among them are forty donors who pledge a specified amount each month. This income is as dependable as an endowment, and is used to meet our monthly expenses for food and maintenance. Whenever a need arises the funds are available. The generosity of our friends allows us to receive into our home residents who have very little income. Without this help, required residency fees would have to be collected. This would mean the denial of housing for handicapped whose needs are the greatest.

Our home is kept operating with the help of many volunteers. At the top of our list are two Mercy nuns, Sisters Beata Gibbons and Maude McGreal. They were prayer partners before the home opened. Now they both are spiritual and physical workers on hand for all special activities.

Bob and Jack Kramer, two of my nephews roll up their sleeves one Saturday a month when they report for work at the Shelter. Because the weather is so inviting on their work day, their volunteer day at our home is now called "Aunt Rose Saturday." I just tell them they get double pay from above when the sacrifice is the greatest.

Volunteer drivers and workers are the ones who make our prayer meetings possible. I couldn't afford to pay for their services if they were on salàry. I've placed them on God's payroll.

The Shelter of God's Love Board of Directors are another "behind the scenes" VIPs. They have spent many hours working on newsletters, legal matters, fund-raisers and involvement with the residents. Two not previously mentioned in the book are Jeannette Cavender and Ray Nickels who spend considerable time volunteering services to us in food pick-up once a month and as members of the Admissions Committee. Ruth Crigley and Carter Burton, two other members of the Board, who are themselves handicapped, have helped us considerably by their insight and recommendations for the needs of the residents. Carter is also a member of the Admissions Committee. None of the Board receives any financial remuneration in salary or expense money.

The spiritual help we receive from our own Intercessory Prayer Group and other prayer groups throughout the city keep our needs always before our dear Lord. Many priests, religious and lay communities keep us in their prayers. A special "Thank you" to the elderly and infirm nuns at Mercy Manor in Aurora. They are a power house of blessings for us all.

I pray that all who read this book will seek their help from the same source from which my strength came. There were times when I lost the awareness of His presence in my life, and I found myself crying out for human consolation and sympathy. When I couldn't find it, I begged God to be present to me again. He always responds to my need of Him. I pray that all of you will seek and find Him in your laughter and in your tears, both of which are the substance of life.